Life into Story

Life into Story

The Courtship of Elizabeth Wiseman

MARY CHAN

Ashgate

Aldershot • Brookfield USA • Singapore • Sydney

© Mary Chan, 1998

All rights reserved. No part of this publication may be reproduced, stored in a retrieval system, or transmitted in any form or by any means, electronic, mechanical, photocopying, recording, or otherwise without the prior permission of the publisher.

Published by
Ashgate Publishing Limited
Gower House
Croft Road
Aldershot
Hants GU11 3HR
England

Ashgate Publishing Company
Old Post Road
Brookfield
Vermont 05036-9704
USA

The author has asserted her moral right under the Copyright, Designs and Patents Act, 1988, to be identified as the author of this work.

British Library Cataloguing in Publication Data

Chan, Mary
    Life into Story: The Courtship of Elizabeth Wiseman.
    (Women and Gender in Early Modern England, 1500-1750)
    1. Wiseman, Elizabeth—Correspondence. 2. Courtship—England—
History—17th century. 3. Women—England—History—Modern
period, 1600- . 4. Women—England—Social conditions.
5. England—Social conditions—17th century.
I. Title.
941'.067'092

ISBN 1-84014-212-X

Library of Congress Cataloging-in-Publication Data

Chan, Mary
    Life into story: the courtship of Elizabeth Wiseman / Mary Chan.
    p. cm.
    (Women and Gender in Early Modern England, 1500-1750)
      Includes bibliographical references and index.
      ISBN 1-84014-212-X (hb)
    1. Marriage—England—History—17th century—Sources.
2. Courtship—England—History—17th century—Sources. 3. England—
Social conditions—17th century—Sources. 4. Wiseman, Elizabeth,
1647-1730—Correspondence. 5. Elite (Social sciences—England—
Correspondence). I . Title. II. Series.
HQ615.C48   1998
392.4'0942'09033—dc21
                                                                                          97-50361
                                                                                              CIP

ISBN 1 84014 212 X

This book is printed on acid free paper

Printed in Great Britain by Galliard (Printers) Ltd, Great Yarmouth

Contents

Acknowledgements   x

Introduction

1. The story and its significance   xi
2. The documents as historical data   xviii
3. Marriage and the law in the 1680s   xxvii
4. The documents as evidence and as story   xxxiv
5. Editorial   xliv

The Documents

1. 1686 The Journall of the buissness of Spencer as it happned in time   1
2. Mr Chute's Relation   2
3. Lady Wiseman's letter to Sir D. North Sept. 27 '86   6
4. Lord North's letter to Lady Wiseman 1 Oct. 1686   7
5. 11. Oct. 1686. Memoriall Concerning sister Wiseman A Relation of what hath passed within my knowledg and observation concerning the pretences of Mr Spencer to my sister, the Lady Wiseman. 11 Oct. 1686   9
6. Lord North's letter to Lady Wiseman 13 October 1686   14
7. Letter to sister Wiseman about Sir Jo. Thorold 14 Oct. 1686   15
8. Message from Sir Jo. Thorold 16 Oct. 1686   15
9. Memorandum of Sir John Thorold's visit. 19 Oct. 1686.   16
10. Narrative of Sir D. North relating to the Lady Wiseman 22 October 1686   18
11. Copy of a letter to Sir G. Weneev, about Sr. Wiseman   22

vi CONTENTS

12	The Lady Wiseman's relation concerning Mr Spencer. Oct. [1686]	23
13	Copy of our first letter to Sister Wiseman at Brettenham, [27] Oct. 1686. (also 14)	27
15	From Lady Wiseman 2 Nov. 1686	33
16	Letter to Lady Wiseman 6 Nov. 1686	34
17	Sis. W's letter. Nov. 10 1686 received	36
18	Discours concerning Lady W. 8 Nov. 1686	37
19	10 Oct [i.e. Nov.] 1686 discourse with Lord North about sister Wiseman	39
20	Letter from Roger North to Elizabeth Wiseman 10 November 1686	39
21	Letter to Mr Oliver from John Fortescue 11 November 1686	43
22	Letter to Elizabeth Wiseman from Dudley North, Mountague North and Roger North 12 November 1686	43
23	Robert Foley somewhat touching Lady W. Nov. [13] 1686	45
24	Lady Wiseman's letter to DN 8 [i.e. 15] Nov. 1686	46
25	Copy of Sis. Wiseman's letter to Lord N. Nov. 15 1686.	47
26	Copy of Lord N.'s letter to Sir Hen. North 16 Nov. 1686.	49
27	For the Honourable Lady Wiseman at Sir Georg Weneev's hous in Brettenham 18 Nov. 1686	51
28	Narrative upon delivery of the letter to the Lord North 19 Nov. 1686	52
29	Letter to Lady W. 20 Nov. 86.	54
30	Lord North's letter 20 Nov. 1686	56
31	Robert Foley, somewhat touching Lady W. Nov. [22] 1686	58
32	Lady Wiseman to us 22 Nov. 1686	59

33	Letter to Lady W 23. Nov. 1686	60
34	Letter to Lady W. 25 November 1686	63
35	An account of what past between me and Mr Spencer, and between Mr Spencer and Mr Chute as I had the same upon discours with him afterwards the same day viz., Thursday Nov. [25] 1686	64
36	Letter from sister Wiseman 29 Nov. 1686	67
37	Letter for Lady Wiseman 2 Dec. 86	69
38	2 letters from an unknowne freind [letter 1, 4 December 1686]	70
39	M.N.'s account of his visit 5 Dec. 1686	71
40	The second letter [6 December 1686]	72
41	Letter from Elizabeth Wiseman to Roger, Dudley and Mountague North, 6 December 1686	73
42	Letter from Roger North to Elizabeth Wiseman 9 December 1686	75
43	Letter to Lady Wiseman 9 December 1686	81
44	Lady Wiseman 14 December 1686	84
45	Letter from Dudley North, Mountague North and Roger North to Elizabeth Wiseman [14] December 1686	88
46	Letter from Elizabeth Wiseman 21 December 1686	92
47	Mr White Dec. 29 [i.e. 26] 1686	94
48	Oxenbridges Note 7 Apr. 1687	95
49	Letter to the Earl of Yarmouth from Charles North 3 May 1687 (also 50)	96
51	The passage at Lord Yarmouth's with Lord North 8 May 1687	97
52	Sir H. Beddingfeild May 1687	97
53	Bond of Mr Spencer to the E. of Y	98
54	Spencer's Releas to Mr P. and Mr R.	99
55	Sir H. Beddingfeild 16 June 1687	100

56	Letter to the Earl of Yarmouth from Robert Spencer 7 January 1689	101
57	Lord Yarmouth, Jan. 1689	102
Bibliography		105
Index of Names		111

Women and Gender in Early Modern England, 1500-1750 General Editors' Preface

Foregrounding women and gender has become one of the most vital and revolutionary means for reinterpreting the early modern period. Study of the period through the doubled vision of gender has been the source of some of the most original and lasting challenges to orthodox readings of the period. We hope that 'Women and Gender in Early Modern England, 1500-1750' will act as both a continuation and a spur to this movement.

The dominant focus of the series is early modern England, but within that parameter our intention is for the series to be sufficiently open to allow it to respond flexibly to the shifting complexities of the field. Accordingly, no methodology or specific theoretical orientation is prescribed or required, and the series encourages approaches from all disciplines and is especially open to interdisciplinary studies. Despite its rubric, the series is not limited strictly to monographs, and will include editions and collections of essays as well.

'Women and Gender in Early Modern England' is also not limited to the subject of women's writings reproduced in 'The Early Modern Englishwoman: a Facsimile Library of Essential Works', although this is one of the areas we hope to see explored. We hope that this series will capture the energy of the many scholars who are enthusiastically engaged in the reinterpretation of the period, and that 'Women and Gender' will in time become, like its sister project, 'a library of essential works' for the study of early modern women and gender.

Betty S. Travitsky and Patrick Cullen

Center for the Study of Women and Society,
Graduate Center, City University of New York and
Ph.D. Program in English, Graduate Center,
City University of New York

Acknowledgements

I came across the documents in this volume while I was gathering material for my edition of Roger North's *Life of the Lord Keeper North*. Many of the documents owned by Dr Thomas North belonged to Roger North (1651-1732) who purchased the Rougham estate in 1691 and it is among these papers that the present documents are to be found. As far as I am aware, the presence of the documents for the case of Elizabeth Wiseman among the North papers was unknown until I came across them recently. I am most grateful to Dr Thomas North for permission to go carefully through his papers and to publish these documents. I should also like to thank Mrs Pamela North for her hospitality and generosity on my several visits to Rougham over the past years.

Dr Lyndy Abraham gave me invaluable assistance in glossing historical usage in the text and in proofreading. I should like to thank her for this, for her encouragement and enthusiasm and for her insight into the life of Elizabeth Wiseman.

Introduction

1. The story and its significance

Among the manuscript papers of the North family at Rougham Hall in Norfolk is a collection of letters and first-person narrative accounts relating to the courtship of Elizabeth Wiseman (née North) by Robert Spencer in 1686-87. The collection was made by Elizabeth Wiseman's brother, Roger North (1651-1734), a lawyer and, in 1686, Attorney General to James II's wife, Queen Mary. He preserved letters relating to the case and wrote his own account of it. He also had other members of his family who had anything to do with the affair write accounts of incidents which had bearing on Spencer's courtship because the matter became a legal battle in which North acted for his sister. Two other brothers also assisted Elizabeth Wiseman during the affair, and indeed letters to her which are preserved are usually from all three. These were an older brother, Sir Dudley North, in 1686 Commissioner for Customs, and a younger brother, Mountague North, a merchant then residing in London.

The documents as a whole are important for several reasons. First, they represent an almost complete correspondence on the topic of courtship and marriage, a correspondence which includes a number of people all with strong interest in the outcome. This is not a correspondence about love, or between lovers; it is, rather, about indifference, dislike and, eventually, fear. It is about the social and legal constraints and, for some parties, the possibilities for wealth and status, of matrimony at the end of the seventeenth century. Second, all the participants in this correspondence were people of influence and social standing in London of the 1680s and Elizabeth Wiseman's courtship and possible marriage were a matter for gossip and public discussion. Third, the documents provide historians with a glimpse, usually unavailable from other sources, of the rich and complex texture of social life in the brief time they cover. This insight includes family relationships and the private thoughts and feelings of people who would not - apart from personal letters - have left an account of them, besides the wider social issues of arranged marriages, marriage contracts and the perceived dangers waiting to trap the wealthy widow. But perhaps most significant for twentieth-century and accidental readers of these documents (for they were never intended to reach a reading public, beyond their possible use in court) is the transformation of this incident (momentous while it took place) into a narrative by the cumulative form of the collection: the transformation of life into story.

Elizabeth Wiseman (4 January 1647-23 January 1730) had been widowed at the age of thirty-seven on the death of her first husband, Sir Robert Wiseman, in 1684. She had been left with a fortune of approximately £20,000.[1] When she was introduced to Spencer in September 1686 by her eldest brother Charles, Lord North and Grey, and his wife, Lady Katharine North, she claimed that she 'lik'd him so ill' that she asked her servants not to admit him again. Some days after this first visit, Elizabeth Wiseman's sister-in-law, Lady Katharine, asked to bring a friend to visit her, but did not name him. The 'friend' turned out to be Robert Spencer, and consequently, Elizabeth received him 'coldly'. Lady North was annoyed at this reception of her favourite, telling her sister-in-law that Spencer had a fortune, that he was in love with her, and that he wished to marry her. She invited Elizabeth to dinner the next day, an invitation Elizabeth wished to refuse because she 'was afraid Spencer would be there'. Lady North would not accept the refusal, and consequently Elizabeth went to dinner. Spencer was present; and at the same dinner an arrangement was made with Elizabeth that she would accompany her brother and sister-in-law to their house at Tooting the following day 'to eat grapes there'.

The next day Elizabeth persuaded her cousin, Thomas Chute, who called to see her in the morning, to go with her on this trip to Tooting, fearing that she would be left alone in the garden with Spencer. This in fact did happen, although the garden was sufficiently small to allow all that went on to be observed, if not heard, by the others. They each gave different accounts of what they saw, particularly about whether Spencer had or had not kissed Elizabeth on the balcony of the house.

---

[1] The marriage with Sir Robert Wiseman, Dean of the Arches, had been arranged by Elizabeth's brother, Francis North. In North, Roger (1995), p. 192, Sir Robert is described like this:

> He was an old man but very rich, and withall a most just and good natured person. He made no other setlement, then by a bond to leav her portion [i.e., Elizabeth's portion of £1500] doubled, and sayd that it not being prudent to exceed the ordinary measures in those cases, he would doe no more, but he would not have it thought his intentions were confined to that; and after divers years living very happyly together, he left her at his death near £20,000.

Elizabeth was so annoyed at being trapped in this way that she went next day to her brother and sister-in-law's to complain. While she was there, Spencer came in, and she was left alone with him. He then refused to allow her to leave the room for several hours. After this Lord North and his wife claimed, with Spencer himself, that Elizabeth had agreed to marry him, a claim which Elizabeth herself strongly denied.

As a consequence of this claim, Elizabeth retired to the house of her sister (Christina) and brother-in-law, Sir George Wenyeve, at Brettenham in Suffolk, fearing that Spencer might make good his threat to carry her away by force from her house in London. During this time she received three other offers of marriage: from Sir John Thorold (an offer she seriously considered until Spencer put an end to the marriage negotiations by visiting Sir John and claiming Elizabeth was his wife), from Mr Danvers, and from Mr Neal (who was allegedly already betrothed to, and living with, another woman who wrote anonymously to Elizabeth begging her not to listen to Neal's offer). Eventually, on 10 March 1687, Elizabeth Wiseman married William Paston, 2nd Earl of Yarmouth.[2]

Legal action had been threatened early in the affair with Spencer. When Elizabeth made clear that she would have nothing to do with the proposals of either Spencer himself or of her brother Charles, who was promoting the match, Spencer threatened to sue not only Lady Wiseman for breach of contract but also three of her other brothers (Dudley, Roger and Mountague North) who, Spencer claimed, were supporting her in her refusal of him by slandering him and his reputation.

Robert Spencer had some social and political influence. He was a cousin of Robert Spencer, 2nd Earl of Sunderland, who was a Catholic, powerful in the court of James II; and he had allegedly promised Charles North that if he supported and promoted his suit to his sister not only Charles, but others of the North family, would be rewarded by titles and offices. At one point the Earl of Sunderland involved himself in the affair by writing to the North brothers, Dudley and Roger, requesting them to support his

---

[2] The marriage settlement with the Earl of Yarmouth was arranged by Roger North and Elizabeth Wiseman's lawyer, Mr Soresby, who is mentioned frequently in the Rougham documents. A copy of the settlement survives among the documents in the library of Dr Thomas North, Rougham Hall, Norfolk. Elizabeth's jointure was to be £1100 per annum. On marriage settlements in the seventeenth century see Erickson, Amy Louise (1990). Charles North claimed that Spencer had said that Elizabeth could keep all her fortune if she married him: see Document 4.

cousin's suit. Accordingly, when Spencer's suit was unsuccessful and he threatened legal action for breach of promise, he was taken seriously by Roger North.

The possibility of legal action by Spencer prompted Roger North to suggest that his sister might begin her own action: for iactitation of marriage. Such actions were brought when a person had falsely given out that he or she was married to another, and this second person then sued for an order enjoining silence on the matter. The North brothers advising their sister were wary of taking such an action, for even that, in itself, would draw attention to the family and make them the objects of common gossip. It seems to have been Paston himself who finally took an action against Spencer, in June 1687, after he had married Elizabeth. Spencer then agreed to relinquish all claims to her. Nevertheless, eighteen months later, in January 1689, Spencer sent a challenge to the Earl of Yarmouth claiming that the earl and his brother Thomas, who was a military man and who seems to have involved himself by harassing Spencer, had treated him abominably and that he wanted 'satisfaction'. The Earl of Yarmouth did not know whether to treat this seriously or not and wrote to ask Roger North's advice. This is the last surviving document in the affair: we do not have North's answer.

Because of the seriousness of Spencer's threat, and because of the possibility of a case for iactitation of marriage, Roger North - acting as legal adviser to his sister as well as protecting her as a brother - made sure that he collected, over the six months during which Spencer's suit was pursued and his claims pressed, all documents and first-hand accounts of meetings and words exchanged relating to the affair so that they could be used as evidence if the case came to trial.

Many documents relating to the affair, therefore, survive in the papers of Roger North's descendants at Rougham Hall. Because they were, mostly, carefully dated in order to preserve their value as evidence, they can be arranged in chronological order. Those that are not dated can be placed almost certainly within the sequence from their subject matter and from internal references. When the documents are ordered, what one has is a narrative of the whole affair, consisting of letters interspersed with accounts written as personal records. This narrative includes not only accounts of what various people involved in the affair witnessed or believed had happened, but also the complaints of Elizabeth Wiseman herself against the behaviour of Spencer and Lord North and his wife; the encouragement, and then threats, of Lord North to his sister; the constant encouragement and moral advice which her three supportive brothers, Dudley, Roger and Mountague gave her, particularly after she had moved to Brettenham in Suffolk to stay with her sister's family when Spencer threatened to kidnap her from her house in London; accounts of *other* proposals of marriage during the course of Spencer's suit; accounts of court gossip about the affair; and the advice of her aunt, Lady Dorothy Dacres, to brave out all gossip and come back to London.

* * *

The documents provide material for 'micro-history'. As such I concede that my study of them might be subject to the possible claims against all such history: of concentration on too much detail or too small an episode to be of historical significance. I would claim, conversely, that the documents make available - precisely *because* of their detail, their recounting of a specific series of related events and their restricted time frame - historical evidence that is not available in sources or studies which engage in a larger sweep (of time or subject matter).[3] By allowing us to concentrate on a single (and singular) event and reactions to it, the documents give both a detailed picture of social behaviour, conversation and gesture at this time[4] and evidence for a number of issues of larger historical significance for our understanding of the latter years of the seventeenth century and the early eighteenth century. Among these issues are the legal and social status of women, and of widows in particular; the changing laws of legal evidence; and the attitudes of, and towards, one of the most prominent London families in this period. The documents, read as a sequence, constitute intersecting threads within a web of discourses. These will be severally examined in the sections of the Introduction which follow.

The case of Elizabeth Wiseman and the manner of its record are, then, significant for a number of reasons. One of these is the light it casts on legal matters in the mid-1680s. Spencer claimed that a contract had been made between him and Elizabeth on what now appears to be the flimsiest of grounds - viz., a verbal contract

---

[3] The advantages and disadvantages of the method are discussed by Carlo Ginzburg and Christopher Marsh. See in particular Ginzburg, Carlo (1986), pp. 16 and 164; Marsh, Christopher W. (1994), p. 11 which discusses the methods.

[4] The large amount of direct and reported speech and reporting of physical gesture and action in the letters and accounts not only makes them very lively but, in particular, draws attention to the closeness with which the Restoration theatre reflects contemporary style in social interaction.

allegedly witnessed by two people, Charles Lord North and his wife, Lady Katharine. Elizabeth claimed that no such contract had taken place; but the fact that a verbal contract with two witnesses was considered sufficiently binding to pursue it in a legal action suggests that the matrimonial law of contract was still valid.[5] As material to be presented in evidence, the documents are further significant for the history of the evolving laws of legal evidence at the end of the seventeenth century.

The material relating to the case also documents social behaviour in London in the late seventeenth century, not only the attitudes of the law and society to the remarriage of rich widows, but also, more specifically, the point of view of her immediate family and of the rich widow herself. Barbara J. Todd has made the point that towards the end of the seventeenth century remarrying widows were regarded more critically than they had been earlier in the century. Nevertheless, while the Church was somewhat critical of remarrying widows, there was also social pressure against unmarried widows' freedom from male control.[6] Within Elizabeth Wiseman's family, attitudes are ambiguous. When the Spencer affair begins to be recorded, her three supportive brothers are negotiating a marriage settlement for her with Sir John Thorold. Her eldest brother, Charles North, wants her to marry Spencer because of the specific advantages to himself which he believes will flow from that marriage; and at the same time he accuses his younger brothers of trying to prevent her marrying (Spencer or, presumably, anyone else) because, he claims, they want her wealth kept in the family.

The letters in themselves thus reveal both the different social and familial relationships among the correspondents; but they also draw attention to personal characteristics, styles of response and public and private attitudes. In a period when letters are one of the major forms for women's expression of a 'self' in literature, the letters of Elizabeth Wiseman are significant for the way in which the variety of roles she apparently saw herself required to adopt (for her) constituted this self. For instance, although Charles Lord North casts his sister as the willing, but flirtatious, heroine of a romance, Elizabeth, on the contrary, never appears flirtatious in her own writings. When she writes to the three brothers who are advising her in the affair (Dudley, Roger and Mountague), she adopts a submissive and formal style in reply to their advice; but

---

[5] Stone, Lawrence (1979), p. 30.
[6] Todd, Barbara J. (1985), Boulton, Jeremy (1990), and the reply to this: Todd, Barbara J. (1994).

she also shows her position as elder sister to Roger and Mountague, and is sometimes bantering and familiar. Because she seems at ease with these brothers, her letters, more than any of the others', express a free play of thought and feeling, continually shifting from formal to playful to serious to personal. The letters, taken together, form a contrast with the narratives which are accounts of events and the writers' observations on, and interpretation of, them. The most vivid contrast is between Elizabeth's own narrative account of the events of the case (written about two months after the affair began) - a spirited, direct and confident account - and her letters written throughout the stress of the affair with Spencer which show the day-to-day emotions of self-doubt, annoyance - even anger - and also good humour.

Besides the interest the documents hold for social historians, they provide material of interest for literary historians too. When the documents are taken together they compose a story; and this story element is not accidental. Roger North, acting as Elizabeth Wiseman's lawyer, with the possibilities of legal action (initiated either by Spencer or himself) in mind, kept the letters and requested the various narrative accounts from those concerned, *in order to* create a plausible (and legally defensible) story to produce in court if required. The narrative which the record itself constitutes comes close - to modern eyes - to literary forms of the late seventeenth and early eighteenth centuries: in particular, to the novel. In its closeness to this, the form of the complete narrative draws attention to the relation contemporary novels might bear to the documentation required by legal evidence, and to the ways by which contemporary and early eighteenth-century novels (often composed of letters, purported memoirs and first-hand accounts) were at pains to assert their 'truth'. Thus, while the documents provide details of many aspects of late seventeenth-century customs, beliefs and social interaction, their greatest interest, perhaps, lies in their exemplification of what Natalie Zemon Davis has referred to as 'fictional' elements, the 'crafting of tales' from real events.[7]

---

[7] Davis, Natalie Zemon (1987), *Fiction in the Archives*, pp. 3 and 5.

2. The documents as historical data

The historical commentary provided by the documents (on the social role of a wealthy widow, family relationships, social customs of courtship, marriage arrangements) cannot be considered apart from the form in which the data survive: letters and first-person narratives of events. The letters in themselves provide a different kind of evidence from the documents which were written to record events in the affair as they were perceived by one or another of the actors. There are two obvious reasons for this: first, the accounts of incidents were written with no particular addressee in mind and they were written to provide evidence of the writer's opinion of what happened. Some, such as Thomas Chute's account of the visit to Charles North's house at Tooting (Document 2) were written quite a long time after the events which they narrate, and obviously with the benefit of hindsight. In the case of Thomas Chute's narration, Elizabeth Wiseman had already remarried by the time he came to write his piece. The letters, on the other hand, although written with varying degrees of deliberation, contain nevertheless more immediate reactions to events and affairs of the moment. Elizabeth Wiseman's letters, particularly, are reactive, reflecting her role in the whole affair: to play a part set for her by her rank in society, her position in her family, and her social status as widowed, wealthy and a woman. By contrast, the letters which Dudley and Roger North write to their sister are often carefully contrived, instructive pieces, written with an eye to the consequences of their advice and their writing. This means that Elizabeth's letters, more than those of the other correspondents, provide a detailed insight into her position, the ways in which she saw herself, and herself-as-letter-writer.[8]

Ruth Perry, in *Women, Letters, and the Novel*, discusses the various letter-writing manuals and the styles they advocated. Letters between friends and close family members were not to follow the more formal styles of the various letter manuals but rather to have ' "an easiness of stile" ' which was 'marked as the only mode suitable for writing or speaking the truth'.[9] For letters by both men and women the conventions were in many ways similar: brevity, profession of friendship, concern for the reader. But Patricia Meyer Spacks points out that women's letters, more than men's, seem dominated by conventions. Writing of the

---

[8] For a discussion of the differences between letters and memoirs see Perry, Ruth (1980), pp. 120-21.
[9] Perry, Ruth (1980), p. 74.

letters of the early eighteenth-century writer, Mary Delany, she says:

> Women's letters almost ritualistically apologize for their own length; they reiterate ardent professions of friendship ... The stylized aspects [Delany's] letters share with those of other women express their status as communications dominated by consciousness of *the other*. Hence the special importance of self-subordination: concern for self must not be allowed to block sensitivity to the imagined needs of the recipient.[10]

Elizabeth Wiseman's letters illustrate all these characteristics; and consequently their value as expressions of self or personality is far more entangled with unwritten, and even unacknowledged, attitudes than the letters of her brothers (apart from those of Charles) which, because of their role in the affair as conveyers of information, as authoritative and advisory, seem more frank.[11] To a modern reader, Elizabeth's letters seem, more obviously than theirs, the expression of meanings which are culturally defined. This may be partly because of her social position and because she is a woman: she is both the subject and the centre of the whole affair, and yet unable to act on her own. And yet again this may be simply an aspect of her individual personality, her own reaction to her present situation.[12]

Elizabeth Wiseman's letters are mainly a consequence of her retirement to Brettenham, in Suffolk, to stay with her sister Christina Wenyeve until the affair with Spencer had blown over. The documents contain only one letter written from her house in London (Document 3) and this is a brief and early piece, informing her brother Dudley (on his arrival in London) about the Spencer affair so far. We learn more about Elizabeth and her reaction to her socially imposed position from the later letters, from Suffolk. But even in this early letter to Dudley North we see expressed her antipathy towards Spencer and his suit from which she never

---

[10] Spacks, Patricia Meyer (1988), p. 181. See also Würzbach, Natascha (1969), p. xiii.

[11] This is only an appearance (and by contrast) to modern readers. Roger North refers to the artifice of letter writing in Document 33 when he writes of the present necessity for seriousness, for writing in a style 'not such as wee have bin alwais so free to use, as freinds, with mixture of earnest, the more divertingly to insinuate our sence'.

[12] In a single case like this generalizations are neither possible nor desirable. For the use of autobiographical writing as historical evidence see Graham, Elspeth, Hilary Hinds, Elaine Hobby and Helen Wilcox eds (1989), pp. 17-18.

changes. Her wish that Dudley might join her in her visit to Charles North 'that you may take a view of this hobby horss, that we may haue something to laugh at next meeting' confidently mocks at Spencer and his pretensions; later this mockery turns to defensiveness when his claims on her become more menacing and she realizes that she must take him more seriously. In the letters from Brettenham, Elizabeth's attitude to Spencer fluctuates between jesting about him as one of her many suitors and anger at Spencer for forcing her to leave London for the country. Both attitudes can be read as defensive; but the bravado with which she expresses her annoyance at Spencer's threats also draws attention to the fact that she is (as letter writer) writing to impress an audience. She appears to need to impress her brothers with her stoicism, a reaction to her clear irritation at her socially enforced passivity. An example is her outburst in Document 44 in which she says

> I defy the divill and all his works. Lett him do what he can, and when I come to town if he dares come neer me Ile spit in his beastly face.

Roger North comments on this forced style in her writing when he replies to this (Document 45):

> wee are glad to find such a bon courage as you shew, which in good earnest is one very considerable peice of armour. But in the maine wee expected that you would have those sentiments you express. Wee have already say'd what is proper in answer, which is in short that your owne heart is your guid, and you have reason to move in your owne best approved methods, wee hoping you will find all content, soe much the more by that hearty swaggering.

Elizabeth's attitude to her brothers appears all the more clearly an imposed role when considered beside the frank and straightforward account she writes in October 1686 of the affair so far.

Behind their assumed attitude of defiance Elizabeth Wiseman's letters reveal a woman of good humour and much sense, but they also show her trapped in the conventions of her situation. She can write of her own letters as if they were insignificant: that she 'cares not who sees [them] being only of course and civility', but they inevitably show more of her in her social role than she would claim. She defers to the masculinity and wider knowledge of the world of her supportive brothers (two of whom are younger than her). On the one hand she shares with them their jesting over visits from her other suitors (Neal and Danvers) and the harangues of their aunt, Lady Dacres, and she complains about her difficult situation as a long-term visitor in her sister's house. On the other hand she adopts a submissive role in response to her brothers' long moralistic comments and appears to accept these with humility, as for instance in Document 15:

> And in the mean time your letter shall be my study, wherein there are many notable observations, and great truths and I will endeauour to guide my selfe, accordingly for the future.

She also defers to their greater sense of the need for subtlety in writing to her eldest brother, Charles North: for instance, she accepts the letter Dudley and Roger send her to copy out and send on as her own to him (Document 25). Later (Document 32) she says she will again seek her brothers' help in replying to Charles if he writes to her, saying 'where they lie at catch, it tis not safe for me to trust my selfe, and I do suppose I may haue a return by the post soon enough'. At the end of Document 36 she has completely accepted that her letters to Charles North must be very cautiously written and asks directly for a copy to answer him if her brothers think it needful.

While we might see Elizabeth's letters as those of a literate and intelligent woman caught in a difficult situation - forced to leave home and forced to rely constantly on the advice of younger brothers - nevertheless, her brothers see her differently. Roger North draws attention to the brothers' paternalistic attitude towards Elizabeth when he refers (in Document 33) to their correspondence as in part, and earlier in the affair, indulgent and only playfully instructive but, now that Spencer is threatening kidnapping and revenge, needing to be serious and carefully attended to. It is now time for Elizabeth to understand her complex and precarious social position:

> Wee must desire you to excuse the gravity of the stile, for wee doe assure you the matter in hand is neither in jest, nor capable of any, not such as wee have bin alwais so free to use, as freinds, with mixture of earnest, the more divertingly to insinuate our sence.

It is also clear from their moralizing to her and from the way in which they take up her affair that they are doing more than simply advising her, despite their frequent protestations that she is her own mistress and must be ruled by herself. Rather, they see her as weak and defenceless, liable to be imposed on because of a romantic lack of understanding of her worldly situation, unaware of the real dangers lying in wait for her, and unaware of the scandal a false move or idle word might bring upon her whole family. On the one hand, Roger North describes her character to her*self* like this in Document 43 (comparing her with the formidable Lady Dacres):

> Wee now understand that Lady Dacres intends to write about your coming to towne and being of opinion that you may now scorne all things to that degree you master yourself and them. Wee doe not concurre with her in that perswasion; unless you had a double, at least an equall spirit, with hers; your education, nor temper is not that way, having most of the oblidging and complyant.

Later (Document 45), Roger North describes Elizabeth as not being able to 'support such a bravery' as Lady Dacres, saying that she would need 'the exercise of a greater ill nature, and that continually, then you are acquainted with, or in any sort used to'. He goes on: 'But civility and temper which are your vertues, in these affaires are destruction'. On the other hand, when Mountague describes a conversation he had with Charles North about their sister (Document 39), what the brothers describe to *her* as her frank and obliging nature is, among themselves, simply the behaviour of 'a silly [i.e., simple] woman'.

Charles North's letters cast the family's patronizing of their rich, and consequently difficult, sister in yet another light. Even taking into account his (scarcely disguised) selfish interest in setting up the whole affair, he seems to have little regard for his sister or her happiness. His letters, more than those of his brothers who support Elizabeth, draw attention to the gap between marriage as romance (marriage for love, or from choice, which fills the theatre and sells novels) and marriage as a business matter and for social convenience. On the one hand, his letters make clear that his support for Spencer's suit is for his own (and the family's) personal gain; on the other, he characterizes Elizabeth's reactions to this suit as romantic, her behaviour as (expectedly) flirtatious. His sarcasm in this is barely concealed, proclaiming that he writes as he does merely to humour an insipid sister.

The first letter in the series he writes to her (Document 4) adopts an ornate and extravagant style with expressions such as 'when mutuall fyres were raised almost to a flaming abroad', 'geniall raptures' and his description of Spencer as a gentleman of an agreable age, desirable proportion, features, complexion, great in family, weighty in reason, of a smart witt and yett most sedate and sober in life and conversation, with a competent estate and that loves you passionately.

In Document 6 he writes to Elizabeth about the possibility of 'so worthy a servant [dying] upon your damnd usage of him'. Later, in Document 30, when he appears to be more defensive of his behaviour towards his sister, he still writes with extravagance, dismissing his sister's own claims and rights in her choice of a second husband as insignificant. When he speaks to the other brothers, his reported behaviour is that of the bully: cowed and indecisive. His brothers recognize this side of his character. For instance, in Document 5, Roger North writes of a conversation he had with Charles when he faced him with an account of his encouragement of Spencer's claims: 'He say'd he took it that they had bin as good as married, or as it were contracted; (in his doubdtfull hesitating way of speaking in nice concernes).' Later, he tries to make light of his role in the whole affair, referring to Elizabeth as 'sister Wiseacre' (Document 19); and his letter to his cousin, Sir Henry North (Document 26) is defensive of his conduct in the face of reports Sir Henry might have heard elsewhere.

What kinds of historical data can we gather from these documents? Most obviously they bear witness to certain specific legal and social conditions of the 1680s pertaining to marriage and the role of the rich widow. These will be discussed in detail in the next section. But the documents also bear a more subtle witness: this is of two kinds and relates particularly to their central subject, Elizabeth Wiseman herself and the fact that her story survives as letters, rather than in another form. First, her letters fill out and amplify our understanding of late seventeenth-century social interaction: subtle privileges of rank, tones of voice, even details of movement, facial expression, gesture. We see Elizabeth acting within her familial sphere; and reacting to what was one of the most significant means by which society was organized socially and financially: marriage.

Second, we also see, from others' letters, a more objective view of her situation; and, from a modern perspective, her situation is intolerable. She is restricted in her choice of a second husband - in the choice both of *whether* to remarry and *whom* to remarry. Her sister-in-law, Lady Katharine North, allegedly accuses her, in Document 12, of not mixing sufficiently in the world after the death of her first husband: 'she told me I sate mumping by the fyreside and would neuer be well till I came abroad'; and when her supportive brothers are encouraging her to choose for herself they are accused of deliberate lack of direction to her because they don't want her to remarry, so that her fortune will be kept in the family. The documents relating to the on-going courtship of Sir John Thorold (who is finally discouraged from pressing his suit when Spencer pays him a visit, Document 9) make clear that this marriage is to be predominantly a financial arrangement. There is no intimation from Elizabeth about her feelings towards him. Only after he has withdrawn from his courtship can Mountague write to Elizabeth, jestingly, in Document 22, that he

> saw Sir J. Tho. att a play, who has bin asked after you and says he knows nothing of you, nor whither you be or be not in towne. He is the same man I ever saw him and if any thing, more gay and truly methinks he does not seem to pine much for loue, or lay to heart the misfortunes he unknightlike left his lady in and to labor under.

It comes as a surprise that Elizabeth has married William Paston, 2nd Earl of Yarmouth, for there has been no mention of his name. This may be because letters are lost from the sequence, or because Roger North thought them inappropriate to retain for the purposes of legal action with Spencer. There is one possible reference to Paston, but no name is mentioned - indeed a name seems deliberately avoided. If the reference is to Paston, its obliqueness is itself a commentary on Elizabeth's perception of her own role in the arrangements for her second marriage. It occurs in Document 15:

> I presume amongst good people the matching me to that excellent man, will not be at all enjurious nor to my bussiness; and for others, I value them not. I thank you for the care you have of me, and am very well satisfied with your conduct in my affairs, for I am sure you will doe nothing but vpon good consideration.

This seems unlikely to refer to Roger North's investigations on behalf of Sir John Thorold's suit since only a fortnight earlier (Document 9) Sir John had declined to continue negotiations for Elizabeth after receiving a visit from Spencer. If this refers to Paston, the manner of Elizabeth's marriage arrangements shows how small is the part she is expected to play, how much the marriage is for the *family* honour and standing.

When Elizabeth finally marries again, and the affair with Spencer has been brought to a legal settlement, no more is heard of her - in any of the thousands of leaves of writings among the papers of Roger North - nor do letters to or from her survive.[13] Elizabeth was now to live 'happily ever after': other sources inform us that she lived more than another forty years, that she had no children by either marriage, that her husband outlived her by two years and died a bankrupt. Her role throughout the brief affair with Spencer was comparatively passive: she was not free to go about her business, having once said that she was not interested in accepting Spencer's suit. Rather, she was trapped into an appearance of an agreement to marry him (although she herself claimed she said nothing when Charles tried to make her take Spencer's hand), and then she was virtually compelled to imprison herself in the country under the protection of her brother-in-law, escaping from her London house in her brother, Roger's, coach whilst her own waited outside her front door as a decoy.

It would, however, be too easy to read the documents as simply confirming already existing twentieth-century stereotypes of the late seventeenth-century social position of women: excluded from society, repressed and powerless. In some ways, of course, Elizabeth fits the stereotype;[14] but to see only this would be to devalue the subtleties of the letters. Margaret J.M. Ezell has written eloquently on the ways in which historical data on women in the early modern period have been and can be interpreted, and the present documents support her case for a less rigid reading of literary documents by women.[15] She draws attention, for instance, to the ways in which a twentieth-century viewpoint can misread certain kinds of documents, particularly unpublished ones, by taking too restrictive a view of their purpose.[16] She also refers to the work of

---

[13] Roger North mentions this affair with Spencer again in both versions of his Life of Sir Dudley North (1709 and c. 1721): British Library MSS Add. 32512, f. 153 and Add. 32513, f. 122v. In the latter, the section head in the manuscript is 'Defended his sister against a court interest'. The context in both cases is the role Sir Dudley played in the affair, as adviser to Elizabeth, the example he gave of his brotherly support and his standing up to the Earl of Sunderland by not wavering in his intention to pursue a case for iactitation of marriage if necessary.

[14] The late seventeenth-century characterization of women as dissemblers and deceivers and its implications for their exclusion from 'civil society' is discussed by Shapin, Steven (1994), pp. 86-8. This is the way her elder brother, Charles Lord North and Grey, treats her, thus attempting to give credence to his own claims. On the other hand, her supportive brothers treat her with 'civility' but at the same time imply that her position is not a free one - as theirs is, relatively.

[15] Ezell, Margaret J.M. (1993a). See also Ezell, Margaret J.M. (1993b).

[16] Ezell, Margaret J.M. (1993a), p. 146. Ezell refers in a footnote to Bernikow, Louise, ed. (1974), p. 20 and Greer, Germaine et al., eds (1988), p. 20. See also

Lindall Gordon, who has observed of developments in writing women's social history, 'In the history of Women's history, the greatest of our contradictions has been that between domination and resistance' and Ezell goes on to say

> In Gordon's view, women's social history has not yet become comfortable with interpretations of women's lives in the past that include both repression and resistance. To some historians, attention to women's authority in the domestic sphere seemed like 'a romanticization of oppression'; on the other hand, Gordon asserts, 'I still read too many histories of female experience as powerless, which is false and impossible. To be less powerful is not to be power-less, or even to lose all the time.'[17]

'Less powerful' might well describe Elizabeth Wiseman's situation. The present documents are valuable in making this point, partly because of their almost accidental survival and their private nature. While one might claim that they do not represent an entirely repressive culture for women, one might suggest, more accurately, that they illustrate a culture different from one which can be described in terms of freedom or repression. For what the letters reveal - partly by their very personal and detailed expression - causes us to revaluate a dominant view of women as socially repressed, without a voice. There is no doubt that Elizabeth Wiseman's choices are limited and that she sees herself, and others see her, as playing a social role - one to a large degree imposed on her. But the way in which her letters express her perception of her role simply helps to point up the truism that in all periods roles are prescribed for both men and women and for every social class. She recognizes that what is at stake here is not simply personal choice (although her brothers are willing to allow that that is important for her) but rather the family: its honour, its status, its social role. Elizabeth's letters reveal this, even without the clear directions of her supportive brothers. Theirs too recognize this, in that they involve themselves in their sister's affairs not, apparently, out of a sense of patronage or desire to control, but from a more disinterested awareness of the inevitable intertwining of all their lives. This is precisely what Charles North will not acknowledge; and his letters, by contrast with those of the other brothers, illustrate just how far the codes of family honour

---

O'Donnell, Sheryl (1984) and Hobby, Elaine (1988), Introduction.
[17] Ezell, Margaret J.M. (1993a) p. 141. The reference is to Gordon, Lindall (1986), p. 24.

and status can be manipulated for his own ends only. This may be one reason why his letters are so stylized: for him, courtship and marriage are games in which men gain all the prizes. Charles's letters, more than any of the others, fit a modern stereotype of seventeenth-century attitudes to women.

Nevertheless, Elizabeth's letters show not only her awareness of her social role but also a 'self' which shines through and which makes her letters attractive to modern eyes. Sometimes she bows to the prescribed role of dependent woman; but she is also the woman of business (she frequently mentions to Roger, her lawyer brother, arrangements which seem to have bearing on the management of her fortune) and the woman who is aware of intimate and personal family relationships - she is the elder sister bantering her younger brothers, and commenting on the details of the lives of those around her. In the mixture these letters contain of Elizabeth's expression of herself as a family member, and as a self, we glimpse a world which cannot simply be judged in light of a modern concern for individuality and self-expression as all-important. In particular, we see Elizabeth live her life aware of the complexities of her situation - as many literate and intelligent women, whose voices have been lost through historical chance or accident, must have lived theirs at the end of the seventeenth century.

3. Marriage and the law in the 1680s

The documents which survive for this case provide important insights into the laws relating to marriage in the late seventeenth century. The basis of the case prosecuted here seems to have been whether or not Elizabeth Wiseman had promised to marry Robert Spencer, whether some form of contract existed between them. Although Charles North eventually retracted his assertions that his sister had promised to marry Spencer (Documents 49 and 50), claiming in his retraction that while Spencer was 'in my house saying I Robert take thee Elizabeth' it was he, Lord North, who 'stop't his carrier and said matters were not come to that', he nevertheless made these assertions firmly and on many occasions throughout the whole affair.

Spencer's (and Charles North's) claim that Elizabeth Wiseman was contracted to marry him was based on the common-law marriage by verbal contract, a form which was considered legally binding up until Lord Harwicke's Marriage Act of 1753.[18] This was the kind of contract that Spencer claimed existed between him and Elizabeth Wiseman. Spencer used his claim of a contract, and therefore his right to legal control over Elizabeth as his wife, to intimidate Elizabeth and her family in a number of ways. Spencer visited Sir John Thorold (whose negotiations for a match with Elizabeth were going ahead at this time) and told him (in Document 9) that he could not marry Elizabeth because

> that lady was his wife before God, and he must have her; for they were contracted, and he had good wittnesses to prove it, and intended to prosecute at law for her.[19]

Later Charles North embellishes the story by claiming that Spencer had told Sir John Thorold not only that Elizabeth was his wife but that she was 'not fit for any man else to have' (Document 28).[20] Spencer also threatened to 'seize' Elizabeth wherever he met her (Document 13) and later declared 'that no means whatsoever, civil and uncivill will be unatempted' to get Elizabeth into his power (Document 42). Elizabeth expresses her alarm at this threat when she says in Document 44 that

> nobody dares break open my doors, nor take a lady out of her coach in London streets, in the broad day light.

Later, unspecified threats are conveyed through Charles North: in Document 45 we learn that 'his lordship did solemnly declare that some great thing wors then what has hapned to you may fall out in a fortnight, and if it doth he is not to be blamed'.[21]

Because of the threats to Elizabeth, the three supportive North brothers suggest on several occasions that they might take legal action against Spencer to silence him. The suggestion of a counter action is made by Roger North in Documents 13 (and 14 which is a

---

[18] See Helmholz, R.H. (1990), pp. 69-70; Stone, Lawrence (1992), p. 17.

[19] It is interesting to compare Spencer's assertions and consequent claims of authority over Elizabeth with the instance of a reverse situation which is revealed by the 'unknowne frend' who writes to Roger North about Mr Neal, one of Elizabeth's suitors whilst she is in Brettenham. The documents referring to this are 38, 40 and 42, in which the woman who claims to be a friend of the common-law wife of Neal first writes to, and then arranges a meeting with, Roger North. (North suspects she is the wife herself.) Her claim on Neal is exactly that of Spencer on Elizabeth Wiseman: 'she being betrothed to him before God' (Document 42). Unlike Spencer, she appears to feel she has no legal power over Neal, and certainly she cannot resort to violence for redress.

[20] See also Documents 33 and 36 where both Dudley and Elizabeth express their shock at Charles North's words.

[21] Elizabeth dismisses this threat in Document 46.

copy of Document 13), 33, 43 and 44. In the first, iactitation of marriage is specifically mentioned, an action which Dudley and Roger North suggest should be taken in the Court of Exchequer.[22]

Iactitation of marriage was the suit where 'one of two parties has falsely boasted or given out that he or she was married to the other, whereby a common reputation of their matrimony might ensue, and the other sues for an order enjoining perpetual silence on that head that he or she was married to the other'.[23] Such a course (or something like it) was actually taken (by the Earl of Yarmouth after his marriage). North had been very cautious about such a suit (Document 43):

> And as for actions in Doctors Comons to be discharged wee see plainely and the lord declares almost as much, that if you sued they will right downe fall upon your honour, and talk, and it may be swear, at least suggest in wrighting in the court, what to us and your freinds they have onely maliciously insinuated. Which tho never so fals will be an intollerable mischeif.

Nevertheless, among the last surviving documents in the case are two which refer to actions in Doctors' Commons. The first (Document 53) is a bond by Spencer not to sue the Earl of Yarmouth over any supposed 'contract' and the second (Document 54) is a 'release' by Spencer of Captain Thomas Paston (the earl's brother) and a Captain Thomas Rawlens. This 'release' implies (as does Document 52) that Spencer had been harassed by the earl's brother and a fellow soldier.

It seems that the Norths feared not only Spencer's threats of violence in considering their own possible legal action to silence him, but also a legal action by him to claim Elizabeth as his wife. This is not mentioned explicitly in the documents but it is implied in Documents 34 and 35 in Spencer's reported remarks to the Norths' cousin, Thomas Chute. In writing later of the affair, Roger

---

[22] See Documents 13 and 14. Conset, Henry (1685), p. 22, says that a case of iactitation of marriage would be brought before the Court of the Arches. This is discussed further in the notes to Document 13. The brothers' suggestion that the suit would be taken in the Court of Exchequer would be unlikely (see Conset) and in fact this was not what happened. It is possible that North conflates two different kinds of action here: iactitation, which would be pursued in the ecclesiastical courts, and what he later refers to as 'an action at law for damages' (Document 43).

[23] *Mozley and Whiteley's Law Dictionary*, p. 178. When Dudley and Roger North first write about this to their sister (Documents 13 and 14) Dudley says the suit is called 'iactitation or bayling of marriage' and Roger says 'iactitation or boasting of marriage'. See also Helmholz, R.H. (1990), pp. 60-61.

North says that he and his brothers feared an action by Spencer in the High Commission. Had Spencer brought his case there the Norths' worst fears of notoriety and scandal would have been realized because Spencer's cousin, the Earl of Sunderland, was one of the commissioners. The reference to the case is in *The Life of Sir Dudley North*:[24]

> At this time the High Comission Court was on foot, which was terrible to many under matrimoniall claimes, and Lord Sunderland, with his freind the Lord Jeffress, ruled the roast there. And Sir D. North apprehended most of all a citation *in causa contractus* from them. And somewhat came to his ear that gave him caus to suspect it, whereupon much deliberation was had how to have comported in such a case: and thereupon he finally resolved to defend his sister *contra gentes*, and thro all extremity not by fending and proving as some other in their causes had done, but by a protestation to the jurisdiction, as of an illegal court, and upon that point, (if they had so farr drove him), to have staked all his interest at court, being then a comissioner of the customes.[25]

The High Commission, as described by Blackstone, was originally set up by Elizabeth I in 1588 'instead of a larger jurisdiction which had before been exercised under the pope's authority'. Blackstone goes on:

> It was intended to vindicate the dignity and peace of the church, by reforming, ordering, and correcting the ecclesiastical state and persons, and all manners of errors, heresies, schisms, abuses, offenses, contempts, and enormities.[26]

The Commission dealt with ecclesiastical matters: for lay people these were mainly matters relating to bastardy, marriage contracts and adultery. The court was abolished by statute in 1641,[27] but in July 1686, just two months before Spencer began his suit to Elizabeth Wiseman, James II revived the High Commission. W.A. Speck says that 'James set up this tribunal to discipline the clergy

---

[24] British Library MSS Add. 32512, f. 153 and Add. 32513, f. 122v.
[25] Add. MS 32513, f. 122v. At the beginning of the passage North has added 'Court' above the line, presumably as an afterthought. The High Commission was not referred to as a 'court' until after its abolition in 1688.
[26] Ehrlich, J.W. (1959), p. 488.
[27] See Usher, R.G. (1913). Usher does not mention anything about James's revival of the Commission in 1686.

following the bishop of London's failure to silence John Sharp, a clergyman who had disregarded a proclamation forbidding preaching against Catholicism', making the point that the Commission dealt with matters concerning the power of the sovereign including the king's right to dispense with the Test Act. It was, in other words, seen as a means by which James, claiming to be above the parliament, could allow Catholics to gain power and influence and thus it was a political as well as a legal institution.[28]

Why did the Norths fear that Spencer might bring their sister before the revived High Commission? Certainly, the influence at court of Spencer's illustrious relation, the Earl of Sunderland, who had recently become a Roman Catholic, had much to do with their alarm. At one point, the Earl of Sunderland attempted to intervene in the affair, writing to both Dudley and Roger North (Documents 5 and 18). There is also a good deal of evidence that neither he nor the Lord Keeper, Sir George Jeffreys, who chaired the Commission, had any love for the Norths.[29]

One of the Commissioners originally appointed to the Commission in 1686 was the Archbishop of Canterbury, William Sancroft, although Speck says that he 'refused to take his place on it'.[30] At this time, Roger North was Secretary to Archbishop Sancroft, and it may be because of this position that among the North papers in the British Library are documents in which North has drawn in detail the similarities and the differences between the original High Commission and the revived High Commission of James II.[31] Despite the belief (and its continued iteration by historians) that the court did not deal with lay cases, it is quite clear from North's comparison of copies of the Letters Patent to the Commissioners in the first High Commission and those to the Commissioners in the second, that there was, at least in theory (and therefore with the threat that practice might follow), little difference in the roles of the Commissioners for each Commission and their jurisdiction, at least when the Commission was first revived, which was shortly before the affair with Spencer began. It is certainly clear that one of the roles of the Commissioners in James II's Commission was

---

[28] Speck, W.A. (1988), p. 63. Speck repeats the view of the revived High Commission expressed by Ogg, David (1955), pp. 175 and 177 more than thirty years before.
[29] See North, Roger (1995), pp. 108-9.
[30] Speck, W.A. (1988), p. 64.
[31] See British Library MS Add. 32520, ff. 48-61v.

to inquire, heare, determine, and punish all Incest Adulteries, Fornications, outragious misbehaviours and disorders in marriages, and all other greivous and great crimes or offences which are punishable or reformable by the Ecclesiasticall laws of this our Realme. ('The Comision, 2 Jac. 2. 1686' Add. MS 32520, f. 51v)

This is close to the instructions to Commissioners in the High Commission of Elizabeth I,[32] so whether or not James intended his Commission to act in matrimonial causes, the power to do so was certainly vested in the Commissioners. Roger North, in his role as Secretary to Sancroft, had access to the workings of the Commission and his knowledge clearly made him fearful of its power to act in Spencer's case.[33]

Besides the threats of specific legal action (on both sides), other attempts were made to settle the case too. On two occasions, Dudley and Roger North suggest that a letter from Spencer withdrawing his claims about a contract be obtained through Charles North. This is first mentioned in Document 29 as a possibility that Elizabeth herself might initiate. In Document 39 Mountague recounts a meeting he had with Charles North at the playhouse when he suggested directly that Charles obtain 'a declaration under [Spencer's] hand' and Charles agreed to it. However, at the end of the account, Mountague says that Charles visited him two days later to say that 'he could not procure from

---

[32] See British Library Add. MS 32520, f. 49. On ff. 54-55 North has drawn up 'A table of comparison of the two foregoing comissions' in which the similarity in this particular instance is clear.

[33] The last of the documents in the collection of notes relating to the High Commission is 'Some powers in the Comission 2 Jac. 2. for ecclesiasticall affairs distinguish't with reference to the legality of them' (ff. 60v-61v). Here North distinguishes between what he calls 'ordinary' and 'extraordinary' powers of the crown (the 'extraordinary' relating to the 'judging all causes ecclesiasticall whatsoever originally, that are with ordinary jurisdictions') and believes that the statute abolishing the first High Commission also abolished the extraordinary powers. He does say, however, that 'the contrary was feared' (f. 61), implying that these powers were reinstated by the second Commission. This may give a clue to the reason why the Commission was so much feared by the North family in the particular case of their sister, and was also generally hated.

The significance of the abolition of the Commission in 1688 is discussed in the unashamedly Whig tract: 'The King's Power in Ecclesiastical Matters truly stated', in *State Tracts: being a farther collection of several choice treatises relating to the government. From the Year 1660 to 1689. Now published in a body, to shew the necessity, and clear legality of the late Revolution, and our present happy settlement, under the auspicious reign of their majesties, King William and Queen Mary.* London, 1692. This tract makes clear a widespread fear of the Commission and its powers, a fear commented on by both Ogg and Speck as curious.

Spencer the writeing he had promised, Spencer saying he would not giue them ease who had giuen him so much trouble'. When Roger North wrote to Elizabeth about this playhouse meeting between Mountague and Charles (Document 42) he added that 'his Lordship's opinion was that Sp. would never sue'.[34]

On several occasions there is mention of recourse to illegal means of redress. Whilst duelling is never spoken of specifically, this is what Roger North refers to when he writes (Document 33):

> Never any thing yet has happned in any of our experiences of such tenderness as this, both in relation to your well being hereafter ... but also to your, and our honnours, with which it is very hard to comport patiently, if they come to speak plaine, what they now too planely insinuate they mean. Few countrys would bear so much, without what I will not mention. There is no being here [i.e., in London], without the test of violence, or dishonnour, one of which, or both you must pass.

There is also a reference to Lord North's visiting Dudley North 'which wee suppose (he not being at home) was to prevent mischeif' (Document 34); and Elizabeth's reply to this letter warns them 'for god sake take care of your selves', indicating that she sees her elder brother's visit as having the same fearful significance as do her other brothers (Document 36). When Roger North writes (Document 35) of his meeting with Spencer at Westminster Hall he says that Spencer claimed 'he must have satisfaction'. North's reply to this was: 'I answered that if I had aspersed him and his family, he might take his cours, for I would not stirr an inch out of my way for him or any els, and my walks were knowne'. That violence was given and received is clear from Documents 52 and 54 in which we learn that the Earl of Yarmouth's brother and his friend had assaulted Spencer. The last word in the affair was a challenge from Spencer to the Earl of Yarmouth, eighteen months after the bond and release were signed, and in that letter Spencer claims that Thomas Paston (the earl's brother) is still 'affronting' him.

The various legal issues revealed in the documents illustrate the important role marriage and honour played in social relations in

---

[34] Elizabeth Wiseman replies to this in Document 44, vigorously rejecting the suggestion of a letter from Spencer: 'I am sorry Munt as it hapen'd, I ever spoke of a noate under S.'s hand, because 'twill make them apprehend I think need requirs it and [that] he did it as from me, which I am so farr from that I defy the divill and all his works.'

this period.[35] The documents also reflect these as almost exclusively masculine issues. Elizabeth Wiseman's marrying is the centre of many actions, legal or illegal, and of the family honour, and yet she never mentions her own feelings towards this (apart from her detestation of marrying Spencer), nor towards the two suitors (Sir John Thorold and Sir William Paston) seriously presented to her. We do not even know that she had choice in the matter. From the legal point of view it is not she who matters but her fortune.

4. The documents as evidence and as story

The documents relevant to the courtship of Elizabeth Wiseman by Robert Spencer were kept by Roger North in order to provide evidence if the matter came to trial - either in an action taken by Spencer or by the North brothers. The documents as they are preserved draw attention to what would have been considered as evidence at the end of the seventeenth century and, when read in the light of contemporary writings on the subject, they also illustrate the changes in laws of evidence which were taking place in these last decades of the century.

The laws of evidence remained fairly static throughout the seventeenth century:[36] there is little change in substance from Edward Coke's commentary on the Sir Thomas Littleton's *Tenures* (*c.* 1481) in 1628 to Sir Matthew Hale's work of 1685. There is, however, a difference of emphasis, and this change of emphasis is towards interpretation of evidence based on probability.

Under 'Evidence' Coke lists two kinds, viz., witness evidence and documentary evidence.[37] He writes of legal decisions based on probability or presumption not under 'Evidence', but when discussing witnesses and juries. He points out that juries might infer, from both witness and documentary evidence, matters which are not able to be materially proved. He lists three sorts of presumption: violent (which, he claims, 'is manie times plena probatio' i.e., full proof), probable (which 'moueth little') and light (which 'moueth not at all'). When Hale writes, nearly sixty years later, the difference between his and Coke's discussion is that Hale combines discussion of evidence itself with decisions based on it, listing the (same) three kinds of presumption under the heading

---

[35] See also Todd, Barbara J. (1985), pp. 54-6 and 83 and Todd, Barbara J. (1994).
[36] The laws of evidence seem not to have been altered during the radical revision of the laws and the law courts in the interregnum. See Aylmer, G.E. (1973).
[37] Coke, Edward (1629), folio 283a.

'Evidence'. He is still, however, wary of reliance on presumption, requiring material proof for conviction.[38] That reconsideration of presumption and its role in legal judgments was taking place at the end of the seventeenth century, however, is seen by comparison of Hale's work with that of Sir Geoffrey Gilbert, writing only about thirty-five years later.[39] Like Hale, Gilbert combines discussion of evidence and judgments based on it, but he writes a whole volume on the law of evidence, and begins by a reference to the kinds of inference (or probability, or presumption) a jury will draw:

> The first Thing to be treated of, is the Evidence that ought to be offered to the Jury, and by what rules of Probability it ought to be weigh'd and consider'd.[40]

Well before Gilbert's work, even before Hale's book was published in 1685, Francis North,[41] in the sketch of an essay entitled 'Of Evidence', had drawn attention to the ways in which probability would impinge on the presentation of evidence and its subsequent interpretation by a jury.[42] He wrote:

> The question is, what is truth? In a case where wittnesses swear directly contrary to one and other and wherein two great partyes are engaged on either side to support the

---

[38] Hale, Sir Matthew (1736, 1971), pp. 289 and 290, says: 'In some cases presumptive evidences go far to prove a person guilty, tho there be no express proof of the fact to be committed by him, but then it must be very warily pressed, for it is better five guilty persons should escape unpunished, than one innocent person should die'; and 'I would never convict any person of murder or manslaughter, unless the fact were proved to be done, or at least the body found dead'.

[39] Gilbert, Sir Geoffrey (1754). Since Gilbert died in 1726 the work must have been written no later than the early 1720s and so it reflects the law up to that time. See also Shapiro, Barbara J. (1983), pp. 171-93. On pp. 186-93 Shapiro discusses the situation at the end of the seventeenth century in England, noting that credit of witnesses and their oaths were beginning to have less weight than *credibility*. See also Shapiro, Barbara J. (1991), pp. 8-12, and Patey, Douglas Lane (1984). Patey draws attention to Gilbert's borrowing from John Locke in defining probability, but he points out that 'Locke's own attempt to give a philosophic account of the degrees of probability amounts to little more than a repetition of older canons for judging the reliability of witnesses', p. 7. Patey might refer here to Gilbert, Sir Geoffrey (1754), p. 111: 'If there be two Witnesses against two, and no preponderating as to their Number, they are to be weighed as to their Credit'.

[40] Gilbert, Sir Geoffrey (1754), p. 1.

[41] Francis North was Lord Keeper of the Great Seal from 1682 until his death in 1685. He was the second son of Sir Dudley, 4th Lord North, and elder brother to Dudley, Mountague, Roger and Elizabeth Wiseman.

[42] See North, Roger (1995), p. 393.

credit of their wittnesses by what means shall a stranger judg between them to satisfie himself.

He goes on to list under the heading 'Topicks' the following matters which are relevant to the kinds of evidence Roger North obviously had in mind in compiling evidence for the defence of his sister against Spencer:

Credit of wittnesses.
Probabillity of the matter.
Testimony concurrent, temptations, insinuations, education.
Arguments from consequences.
Behaviour of persons accused.[43]

Roger North, commenting on this outline essay 'Of Evidence', makes the point that 'it is the proper buissness of peers, and jurors to trye, not the gramaticall construction of words, which every scool-boy can tell, but the credibility of persons, and things; which requires a collation of circumstances, and a right judgment thereupon ...'.[44] North says 'credibility' here, not credit, implying emphasis on 'probabillity of the matter'.

Contemporary thinking on the laws of evidence is relevant to the kind of evidence that might be produced if either Robert Spencer or Elizabeth Wiseman pursued the disputed contract in a court of law. In a case like this, where there was no material evidence relating to the fact, there was only Elizabeth's word against Spencer's. Who was most likely to be believed? Roger North's 'credibility of persons, and things; which requires a collation of circumstances, and a right judgment thereupon' comes into play in such a case. The documents collected by Roger North might provide, individually and as a whole, just such a 'collation of circumstances'.

Elizabeth claimed that she had never (and would never have) made any commitment to Spencer - by way of marriage or anything else. He, on the contrary (through his go-between, Charles North), claimed that she had not only promised to marry him but that a day had actually been set for the marriage; and furthermore, that Elizabeth's brothers (Dudley, Mountague and

---

[43] It is significant that Francis North appears to separate 'Probability of the matter' and 'Arguments from consequences' from 'Credit of wittnesses'; see Patey, Douglas Lane (1984), p. 7. It is likely, though, that Francis North intended that all these matters should come into play, as Roger North's following comment on the essay suggests.
[44] North, Roger (1995), pp. 392-3.

Roger) were forcing her to deny the contract because they wished to keep her fortune in the family by preventing her from marrying a second time. Roger North, as the lawyer acting for his sister, had to produce evidence that would convince a court of law that his sister (and not Spencer or Charles North) was telling the truth.

The surviving material relating to the case provides evidence of the various kinds thought relevant and permissible for Elizabeth's defence. First is witness evidence, on which the case apparently almost solely relies. The claims of both Elizabeth and Charles North are made in the letters; and while Charles North would, under the old reliance on the credit of the witness, have had more weight on his side, a judgment based on credibility would have taken account of the rash comments he makes when he is angry that his sister is not complying with his propositions, comments which make clear that he has a good deal of interest in Spencer's successful prosecution of his suit. Conversely, the 'credibility' of the evidence for Elizabeth's side of the case is contained in, for example, the ways in which she describes her reception of Spencer: that she left the door of the room open when her sister-in-law visited her with Spencer and then went away leaving her alone with him. She claimed that there were servants constantly in the next room. Another instance is her asking her cousin Thomas Chute to accompany her to Tooting since she feared being left alone with her brother and sister-in-law and Spencer. Chute is then able to describe Elizabeth's behaviour towards Spencer when he saw them left together in Charles North's garden. Throughout the letters and accounts there are many examples which could have been used to suggest the 'credibility' of Elizabeth's story, the probability of her having told the truth when she claimed she wanted nothing to do with Spencer and had never encouraged him.

Second, the documents taken together, rather than simply individually, as a historical account, a narrative of the affair, contain an accumulation and presentation of evidence which comes close to providing circumstantial evidence of the kind Gilbert was later to describe under 'violent presumption': 'that is when circumstances are proved which do necessarily attend the fact'.[45] This kind of evidence is rather more sophisticated than the other kinds: it relies on the presentation of the evidence as a convincing narrative. So while it is nowhere made explicit that the present documents formed part of an actual case, the fact and order of their preservation imply that they were to form the

---

[45] Gilbert, Sir Geoffrey (1754), p. 113.

substance of evidence to be adduced. They thus provide a unique insight into what might have been considered evidence for the defence and the ways in which a convincing case could be made for one party from what might well have been quite contradictory statements.[46]

The documents themselves contain an account of how they might have been used in a legal defence to make a case for the 'probability' of Elizabeth's claims. The Norths' aunt, Lady Dorothy Dacres, a sister of their father, involved herself in the affair when she came to London in December 1686 (Documents 42-46). She is mentioned in Roger North's *Life of the Lord Keeper North* as a formidable woman who was used to insisting on, and getting, her own way. In the present documents, too, her forceful and bullying nature is apparent. When she is told of the problems her niece is having with Spencer's suit she is outraged at the scandal involving the family and inclined to believe Charles North's story, the first account she hears. Dudley North therefore arranges to visit his aunt, armed with (as Roger North describes it in Document 42) 'all his tackling of papers in his pocket' - that is, the papers which form the present collection of documents. Roger North goes on to describe, in a letter to his sister, the meeting between his aunt, Charles North and Dudley, presenting it (mockingly) as a legal trial:

> And such a scene it was, as never did I hear any thing like. The buissness was to fend and prove upon matters of fact, befor the lady D. who sat as judg and you know the lord [i.e., Charles North] never wants matters of fact to alledg. The main of which was that all that he did in the affair of Sp. was at your [i.e., Elizabeth's] desire and direction, that it was not suddainely transacted, but depended a long time; that you were fond etc., stuff you have bin nauseated with too often. There was DN like a lawyer with his bundle of breifs; Say you so quoth he. Here is your owne hand to the contrary, and there is her hand to the contrary, here are dates of letters, and circumstances in wrighting that shews times etc. Every one of which, (and so many and such instances and passages of confusion were there, not

---

[46] The general discussions of evidence referred to apply to criminal trials. Elizabeth Wiseman's case is not of this kind, but the procedures of accusation and defence in the ecclesiastical courts were similar and a defence against Spencer's claims could most forcefully rely on the circumstantial evidence presented by the documents Roger North collected. For an account of the ecclesiastical courts see Chapman, Colin R. (1992).

possible to be particularized or described) made him stare, gape and gogle, and rune to new facts then new answers. So that all the most minute circumstances that really are in your affair, were fully discussed, and proved on your side beyond possibility of denyall.

* * *

It is the documents' coherence as a narrative, their ability to make a plausible story of the whole affair, which is, perhaps, their most striking element for modern readers. This narrative comes close - to modern eyes - to contemporary and early eighteenth-century literary forms: in particular to the epistolary novel. These novels too claimed truth for their stories.[47] But while much contemporary fiction is at pains to claim truth as a ground on which it might be taken seriously,[48] late seventeenth-century writers of histories were equally, it seems, at pains 'to disassociate the veracity of the historian from the imaginative in literature': true history was to avoid 'fables, invented speeches, and other obvious fictions'.[49] Shapiro goes on to say that, above all, history was 'to be distinguished from the pleading of causes, from defense or apology, and from panegyric and invective'.[50] In other words, fiction was seen to be closer to the rhetorical models provided by the law courts than to the more austere model provided by historians. The present documents, retained to make out a case for 'strong presumption', draw attention to a concurrent interest - by lawyers and writers of fiction - in a particular kind of truth: plausibility. This is separate from the claims of each to historical truth, a claim valid, but not in itself sufficient, for the Wiseman/Spencer documents; a claim spurious for the novels, and in the end not really a significant part of their development of an argument about human motive for action. The similarity of the present documents to early epistolary novels lies, then, in their attention to details of personality, of motive, of interest through a

---

[47] For a discussion of the ways by which late seventeenth-century novels claimed authenticity, see McKeon, Michael (1987), chapter 1.
[48] Titles often claim that the following work is 'The history and adventures of ...' or 'The Life of ...'. See also Haywood, Ian (1986), p. 18. The overt linking of the titles of epistolary and first-person novels with historical accounts in this period may have been to distinguish the novel from earlier romance and to give it status as a serious form of literature.
[49] Shapiro, Barbara (1983), p. 247.
[50] Shapiro, Barbara (1983), p. 248.

gradual accumulation of 'evidence' which forms the 'plot' of the case North wishes to make for his sister.[51]

Of all the many (and disputed) influences bearing on the novel at the end of the seventeenth century, two changes in literary fashion towards the end of the century seem relevant to an argument for a more than superficial link between the present documents and contemporary novels. First is the growing interest in collections of letters, as models to copy and then as stories in themselves. Ruth Perry, writing of the link between collections of letters and epistolary novels, has shown how the growing fashion for letter books towards the end of the seventeenth century led from collections of letters on a variety of miscellaneous subjects to linked letters which 'took pains to delineate character (exemplary or otherwise) and sketched in a relationship between two or more people'.[52] Perry points out how letters in some later letter manuals 'are concerned with finding the right tones to embody different shades of sentiment';[53] and goes on to say that these exemplary letters were bound together by a single consciousness and 'serious moral intention'.[54]

The most overt link between letter novels and the kind of use the documents in the Wiseman/Spencer case were to serve is

---

[51] That literary fiction had for long been modelled on the rhetorical styles of the law courts has been demonstrated at length by Eden, Kathy (1986). She discusses the relationship between Aristotle's *Poetics* and *Rhetoric*, the one devoted to his theory of literature, the other to his theory of forensic argument. She makes the point that for Aristotle it is precisely reliance on probability that distinguishes the orator and the tragic poet from the historian. A similar point was made by Renaissance rhetorical theorists: for example, by Sir Philip Sidney in his *Apologie for Poetry* (1595), a work which continued to have influence well into the eighteenth century. A link between the increasing recognition of circumstantial evidence by the courts in eighteenth-century England and fictional narrative is developed by Welsh, Alexander (1992). Welsh writes of the shift in the middle of the eighteenth century to third-person narratives (from those in the first person) and sees this to be related to a shift from reliance on evidence given by witnesses to evidence contained in the plausibility of the 'story' constructed by lawyers, initially for the prosecution, but later also for the defence. The documents in the Wiseman/Spencer case, preserved to make a legal argument, and considered in the light of late seventeenth-century writing on evidence, draw attention to the way in which cases earlier than those discussed by Welsh, while still reliant on witness evidence, nevertheless also admitted credibility, 'probabillity of the matter' or, what the legal writers called *violentia præsumptio*.
[52] Perry, Ruth (1980), pp. 83-4.
[53] Perry, Ruth (1980), p. 88.
[54] Perry, Ruth (1980), p. 90.

found, though much later, in the first letter of Samuel Richardson's *Clarissa* (1747-8):

> Write to me therefore, my dear, the whole of your story from the time that Mr Lovelace was first introduced into your family; and particularly an account of all that passed between him and your sister, *about which there are different reports*; some people supposing that the younger sister (at least by her common merit) has stolen a lover from the elder. And pray write in so full a manner as may gratify those who know not so much of your affairs as I do. If anything unhappy should fall out from the violence of such spirits as you have to deal with, *your account of all things previous to it will be your justification.*[55]

The second change in literary fashion at the end of the seventeenth century which seems to bear on the present issue is the decline of interest in character books.[56] These, which had been popular throughout the seventeenth century, contain short sketches of character 'types', often, but not exclusively, satiric. They exemplify a view of character as fixed and external, a view of the individual similar to that on which the law courts relied when they sought to identify the 'credit' of individual witnesses in order to determine whether to accept the truth of his or her claims. Women, for example, were thought unreliable witnesses.

Both the decline in the popularity of the character books and the replacement of interest in the individual letter as a model in writing by letters linked in a story indicate a shift to a more fluid, subtle, and inward idea of the person.[57] This is a preoccupation also reflected in plays of the late 1680s and 1690s.[58] Increasing attention to subtleties of thought and motive, which is exemplified in the literature of the late seventeenth century, might be seen as parallel to a similar attention, in discussion of the laws of evidence, to the establishment, and argument for, probability, circumstance and motive rather than reliance on a simple statement of fact.

---

[55] Richardson, Samuel (1985), p. 40. The italics are mine.
[56] See Boyce, Benjamin (1967) and (1955); Smeed, J.W. (1985). Smeed points out that the revival of interest and new directions for character books in the eighteenth century came from La Bruyère: see chapter 3.
[57] See Lyons, John O. (1978).
[58] See Zimbardo, Rose (1986), chapter 6. Zimbardo attributes the shift of interest at the end of the seventeenth century to the influence of John Locke (p. 13): cf. Sir Geoffrey Gilbert who cites 'Mr. Locke' in the margin beside his second paragraph, p. 1, in his treatise on *The Law of Evidence*.

The papers preserved for Elizabeth Wiseman's defence might, then, be regarded as a prototypical novel. As in an epistolary novel, individual documents make little evidential point except on details such as dates and times (Dudley North points to this in arguing before Lady Dacres). Furthermore, as in these novels, individual documents were written with a coherent purpose and, when all were preserved in a sequence ordered by Roger North, they created a story of the case - one which amplifies individual character and motive. This is particularly true for those letters of Elizabeth in which we see her trying to adjust, both materially and emotionally, to her role as victim, a role which is antipathetic to her and also places her in some real danger. Like novels contemporary with, or a little later than, these documents (novels often written with a female audience in mind), the documents contain a moral: besides individual letters containing moralistic advice, the plot becomes the moral. The documents overtly point up the defencelessness and the simplicity of a single woman in London and the need for her brothers' material advice and moral guidance in difficult times. In this case, Elizabeth takes the advice and her virtue is 'rewarded' by a suitable marriage. In a way similar to the fictional situations in epistolary novels, these documents are created out of the separation and isolation of the subject, a situation which makes her more vulnerable. Vulnerability is essential in giving purpose to the writing of the letters: it is also this characteristic which forms the basis of the plot of many early eighteenth-century epistolary novels. As in so many novels of the period, the subject-matter is, almost exclusively, courtship and the plot ends in an appropriately sanctioned marriage. Written originally as separate and sometimes instructive pieces, the letters, as they were collected and arranged, provide a cumulative moral for, and commentary on, the story which is being developed. By paying attention to the advice of her three supportive brothers, Elizabeth is an exemplar of womanly virtue, and upholds the values of her family, so sadly disgraced by the eldest brother, Charles North.[59]

---

[59] In regarding these documents as in some respects 'novelistic' we transform Roger North from simply the lawyer for the defence and a writer of letters to an author, in the way in which Michel Foucault defines author in his essay 'What is an author?': Foucault, Michel (1977). See in particular, pp. 123-4:

> We can conclude that, unlike a proper name, which moves from the interior of a discourse to the real person outside who produced it, the name of the author remains at the contours of texts - separating one from the other, defining their form, and characterizing their mode of existence. It points to the existence of certain groups of discourse and

While acknowledging all these similarities between the legal 'proof' and the fictional story's structure, we are still acutely aware that in the present case this is not a fictional life but a real one; that the marriage with which Elizabeth is rewarded was not as idealistic as fiction would have it, that her wealth probably played the major role in the Earl of Yarmouth's proposal and led her later almost certainly into financial disaster. This awareness gives poignancy to Elizabeth's story, and also to the relationship between legal and fictional narratives which Alexander Welsh points to as a significant development in the eighteenth century.[60]

* * *

There is some irony in the preservation, in private hands, of these documents relating to the courtship of Elizabeth Wiseman and the publishing of them in the present form. My (re)construction of the narrative (originally preserved for legal, defensive, purposes) as a 'story' apparently comes close to the use in the mid- to late seventeenth-century of the topos of the 'discovered manuscript'. This was a device by which an author claimed truth and authenticity for a fictional work, stating that it was not newly imagined but rather that the author acted only in a facilitating and editorial role. Even when the topos was not explicitly used, authors like Defoe, for instance, claimed to be only the mouthpiece through which an authentic story was told.[61]

The editing and publishing of the present manuscript narrative recreates this topos. At the same time the original use of the topos is subverted in that I have argued that this narrative may provide evidence not so much (or merely) for the 'truth' of the story, but rather for the growing recognition in the late seventeenth century of the significance of other kinds of truth - in law as in literature: the more subtle truth of probability and verisimilitude.

---

    refers to the status of this discourse within a society and culture. ... [W]e can say that in our culture, the name of an author is a variable that accompanies only certain texts to the exclusion of others; a private letter may have a signatory, but it does not have an author.

[60] Welsh, Alexander (1992).
[61] See McKeon, Michael (1987), pp. 54-7. McKeon argues that the 'discovered manuscript' topos is not so much a 'critique of the claim to historicity' as 'an implicit instance of that claim' (p. 56), and is thus part of the evolution of the fictional narrative from romance to novel. But for a different - and more plausible - discussion of the topos, see Doody, Margaret Anne (1996), pp. 150-51 where she discusses it as a device common in ancient Greek and Roman novels.

5. Editorial

The documents are written on a series of loose sheets or half sheets of paper preserved among the private papers of Dr Thomas North, Rougham, Norfolk. They are stored in file boxes, each of which is numbered. Most are found in Box 23.c.6, in a bundle together (although interspersed with other documents unrelated to this case). One occurs in Box 23.c.5 and the same box contains a document giving details of the marriage settlement for the Countess of Yarmouth.

The principles adopted in editing these letters and documents for publication are set out below. All the writers have their own idiosyncratic way of spelling, punctuating, abbreviating, and laying out the text of their letters and narratives. Of these, spelling has been retained and punctuation also as far as possible, but I have standardized the layout of letters and expanded abbreviations for ease of modern reading.

- Pagination of each letter is given in square brackets and inferred where individual letter writers do not paginate. Where the text transcribed is that of the original letter (rather than a copy made, as is the case with several of Dudley, Roger and Mountague's) the format of short letters is a single half sheet of paper, folded in half with the message contained on the two inner pages and the address on one of the outer pages. Longer letters have been written on a whole sheet which has been folded in half, with the first page being the outside page of the fold, thus allowing three pages for text and the back page for address.
- Some letters have passages underlined and it is not clear whether these underlinings were made by the sender or at a later date, perhaps when the three brothers were preparing their evidence. Such passages have been printed in italic type in the present edition.
- Full stops have been inserted (where they do not appear in the original) after initials.
- Capital letters have been used for all proper names and lower case letters for all other nouns.
- Capital letters have been used for titles followed by a proper noun: e.g. 'Lord North' (but 'his lordship').
- Obvious errors, such as repeated words, have been corrected.
- Abbreviations have been expanded, or altered to their modern form: e.g. 'yo:' for 'you', '&' for 'and', 'vizt.' for 'viz.', 'ye' for 'the'. Abbreviations still in common usage are retained but

punctuated consistently: e.g. 'Mr', 'Dr'.
- Each letter writer has an individual style of punctuation. Elizabeth Wiseman uses a colon both following an abbreviation ('yo:') and where others would use full stops. Sir Dudley North uses almost no full stops, but commas instead, and sometimes indicates a full stop simply by beginning what should be a new sentence with a capital letter. In both these cases full stops have been added without comment in the present transcription, although commas are retained where each uses them mid-sentence. Charles and Roger North's punctuation is close to modern usage at the ends of sentences and is, therefore, retained. Their punctuation mid-sentence is also retained. Where other writers (such as the 'unknowne frend') use no full stops, or use other punctuation where a sentence end is clearly required, a full stop is added without comment. All punctuation within such sentences is retained. Where letter writers use direct speech some indicate this by capitalizing the first letter of the first word, even mid-sentence. This practice is followed here and standardized for all instances.
- Roger North in particular has some idiosyncratic spellings. He often writes 'off' for 'of', 'too' for 'to' and 'there' for 'their'. These have been silently modernized. So too has his use of 'ff' (the old form of capital) for an initial 'f', even when a capital letter would not be required by modern practice. Except at beginnings of sentences or for a proper name, where the double f is transcribed as a capital letter, it has been standardized as lower case. Other spellings, such as the commonly used 'then' for 'than', are retained.
- None of the correspondents divides letters into paragraphs, running one subject on into another without a break. This layout has been preserved in the present edition because it more closely reproduces the conversational and personal quality of the text. That Roger North, at least, regarded it in this light is clear by comparison of his letters here with his more formal writing elsewhere - for example in his *Lives* of his brothers.

The footnotes to the text are of two kinds, those which gloss words or phrases and those which explain references. I consider the latter first. As with all letters written as personal communications not originally intended to be read by anyone other than the named recipients, there are many references which are specific to the private worlds of the writers and their immediate readers. Examples are: the business which Elizabeth Wiseman had with 'mistress Foynes' (Document 12); or the person referred to when she uses the word 'obligement' (Document 44), obviously invoking a family joke; or the identity of Mary Howard (Document 37) who has the toothache and asks for some of Mountague's snuff to cure it. These, and others like them, are specific to the genre and even while we cannot hope to unravel them we acknowledge that their very randomness and obscurity define the genre and remind us of the myriad details of everyday life which the correspondents experience and deal with and which more formal letters would not mention. It is, perhaps, significant that such references occur more frequently in Elizabeth's letters than in those of the other correspondents. This difference reflects the writers' perception of their activity. For the 'men of business' (as Elizabeth Wiseman calls her three supportive brothers) there is a clearer definition of boundaries between public and private, and a greater awareness of the possible public use of their letters in the future than in the letters from their sister. Elizabeth Wiseman's letters move more freely between the immediate business and private reference, acknowledging that, for her, the Spencer affair is far more than a matter of business and allowing her letters to convey the immediacy of her feelings as she writes.

So, while I have left the private world of the correspondents to hint at itself (and by the very fact of its shutting us out to draw to our attention the richness of this genre), I have attempted as far as possible to recapture the public world of the affair, through explanations of such references as can be annotated: those to places, public figures, contemporary events of a less personal nature. One of the reasons for claiming modern significance for the documents is the involvement of the actors in the political and social world of the late seventeenth century. I have included in footnotes some passages which have been deleted in the text by the author. Not all passages are so transcribed: only those which provide information which has not been retained in the recast phrase or passage.

The other kind of footnote is the glossing of words or meanings no longer in current usage. The *Concise Oxford Dictionary* has been used as the touchstone here, so that words and meanings not found there have been sought in the *Oxford English Dictionary* for their historical usage and glossed. The dates that dictionary gives for the known use of a particular word are also cited since sometimes the present work shows earlier or later usage. A later usage of a word might reflect the social status or age of the writer. Other reference works used for glossing and annotating the text are: C.T. Lewis and C. Short, *A Latin Dictionary*, revised and enlarged edition, Oxford 1969; M.P. Tilley, *A Dictionary of the*

Proverbs in England in the Sixteenth and Seventeenth Centuries, Ann Arbor 1950; John B. Saunders (ed.), *Mozley and Whiteley's Law Dictionary*, 9th edition, London 1977; David M. Walker, *The Oxford Companion to Law*, Oxford 1980. Other books and articles cited in the notes are listed in the bibliography.

The titles given to each of the documents in the present edition are, where these exist, Roger North's. Each document has been folded into an oblong with the blank back page facing out and a title written on it. Where the document is also the original letter (and not a copy) and where its address survives, this is transcribed at the beginning of the document. Sometimes the address might have been written on a separate sheet of paper now lost.

The writers often refer to themselves (and to others) by initials: e.g., DN, CN, and these are retained in the texts. I use the spelling of Mountague's name as it occurs in these documents, although in other places (such as Roger North's *Lives* of his brothers, Francis, John and Dudley) his name is usually spelt Montagu or Montague.

The Documents

Document 1
no date
[in Roger North's hand]

1686 The Journall of the buissness of Spencer as it happned in time

Seppt 18 Saturday Night. Sir D.N. came to towne.
19   Sunday evning - he visited Lady W. when the Lady North came in, but he staying longer then she, no discours past.
20   Monday evning - Lady N. renewd her visit to Lady W. and propounded the buissness of Sp. and made an appointment for Lady W. to sup with her on Tewsday night.
21   Tewsday night. She supt and saw Spencer, then forc't to promise to goe to Tooting next day.
22   Wedensday - went to Tooting.
23   Thursday afternoon. Sir D.N. and lady visited Lady W. when she told what had past at Lord N.'s and Tooting and all the circumstances.
24   Fryday. - Lady W. went to Lord N.'s as she affirmed to renounce Sp.
25   Saturday came to D.N. and acquainted him of the ill treatment the day before at Lord North's when Lady North followed her to Sir D.N.'s [in] her sedan.
26   Sunday Lady N. at 9 at night visited Lady W. and brought Spencer into her hous. After which she would not permitt any of them to enter her hous.
[verso of leaf]
Sept. 26 Sunday. M.N. and R.N. were at Sir Francis Lawlys,[1] and Litchfield Cathedrall.
Oct. 2 They arrived in London, and in the afternoon visited Lady W.[2]

---

[1] *Sir Francis Lawly*: he was a second cousin by marriage of the North brothers and of Elizabeth Wiseman. Their mother, Anne North, was the first cousin of Sir Thomas Whitmore of Apley (his father, Sir William Whitmore, was the brother of Anne's mother, Mary Whitmore). Sir Thomas Whitmore of Apley had a daughter, Anne, who married Sir Francis Lawly (or Lawley).

[2] MS follows this with a deleted comment: 'who supt that night all together at R.N.'s hous till ten'.

3   Sunday, they dyned with Lady [W.] and were with her till ten at night, all supping at R.N.'s hous.

[Elizabeth Wiseman told her brother, Sir Dudley North, about Charles Lord North's and his wife, Katharine's, pressing the suit of Robert Spencer when Sir Dudley visited her on Thursday September 23rd, the day after the visit to Lord North's house at Tooting.[3] Because the visit to Tooting was discussed in person there are no letters about it. Nevertheless, it was to be a significant episode in Spencer's courtship, one frequently mentioned by all parties, and one which Charles, Lord North, relied on until the very end of the affair as evidence that Elizabeth was 'in love' with Spencer. For this reason, I have included here, as the second Document, Thomas Chute's[4] account of the visit to Tooting which he wrote in late March or early April of 1687, after Elizabeth had married the Earl of Yarmouth. This account was presumably prepared for evidence in the Court of the Arches when Elizabeth and the Earl of Yarmouth took action against Spencer for iactitation of marriage, and would follow Document 46 in the chronological sequence of the affair.]

Document 2
'Mr Chute's Relation' no date
[in Thomas Chute's hand]

[f. 1] What I remember concerning the Lady Yarmouth and Mr Spencer

Toward the end of August last or the beginning of September I accidentaly went to dyne at the Lady Wiseman's hous. She said words then to me to the effect she was sorry that she was to go abroad as soon as she had dined but my Lord North had been so very importunate with her to go with him and his lady to eat grapes[5] att Tooting (his house) that she could not refuse to go, tho

---

[3] *Tooting*: in south-west London. In 1686 it was rural and parts were thickly wooded.
[4] Thomas Chute was the Norths' cousin, grandson of their aunt, Lady Dorothy Dacres.
[5] *grapes*: The growing of grapes (and other exotic fruit) in London, and even further north in England, in the late seventeenth century was a subject of some interest. Nicolas Fatio de Duillier, a member of the Royal Society, published a treatise in 1699 on *Fruit-Walls Improved. By inclining them to the horizon: or, a*

against her inclinations, for she fear'd one Spencer woud be there, a man whom my Lord North proposed to her every way the most accomplisht in the world but she said she her selfe thought farr otherwise and ask't me if I knew him or not. I told her no. She said he was an ugly fellow (truly I think those were the words) and she beleivd he had no estate tho my Lord North said he had one and twenty hundred pounds a yeare.

I went with my lady in her coach to my Lord North's, and presently Mr Spencer came, as I remember out of the closet in the parlour. My lord's coach being ready and we all going to the doore my Lady W. would have gone in her owne coach but my lord would have her go in his coach with his lady and Mr Spencer so my lord and I went in my Ladie W.'s coach.

All the way my lord talkt how fitt a match Mr Spencer woud be for my Lady W., extoll'd his person incredibly, and for his estate it was one and twenty hundred pounds a yeare. He told me how many happy matches he had made in his life before and hop't this would be the best of all etc.

When we came to Tooting we walkt in the garden and gathred grapes. We endeavourd to leave Mr Spencer with my lady in one of the walks alone, but she still followed us.

Then Mr Spencer came to me and askt me to be his friend in this affaire. He said he had a great passion for the lady and that my Lord North and my Lady North were his friends so he hop't I would be a well wisher or to that purpose. I answerd him that I was a relation of my lady's but pretended no interest[6] in my lady - if my Lord and Lady North were his friends I said he had good wishes enough (or some such words) but I supposed my Lady Wiseman's owne were best of all if he could get them.

After that he held my lady in discourse alone on the other side of the garden (which is so little that one may see if not heare whatever passes) and I remember I saw him pulling of her about to keep her from going from him and she pulling to get from him. We all [f. 1v] look't and saw this, and my Lord North said some such words as these and I think the very same, laughing - Look, Look d'ye see em. Ah rogues.

---

[6] *pretended no interest*: pretend *OED v.* 4. *trans.* professed (*Ex.* 1401-*c.* 1850); interest 1. *a.* legal concern *in* a thing (*Ex.* 1450-*a.* 1860). Chute may be both defining his 'property' relationship to his cousin (i.e., that he will get no personal benefit from her not marrying, a matter which became an issue with regard to the advice her three supportive brothers were giving her) and indicating that he has no influence over Elizabeth (so that it is useless for Spencer to try to make him an ally in his suit).

such words as these and I think the very same, laughing - Look, Look d'ye see em. Ah rogues.

But I thought there was little occasion to think any action there lookt like encouragement for I laught to see how she seemd to despise Spencer's company, leaving of him, and coming to the company.

Presently after that we came into the court where the ballconie is. My Lady W. came to me laughing and ask't me pretty loud How d'ye like Mr Sp. - and I replyd laughing Truly Madam I beleive as well as your ladyship - and some other words we had to that effect which I forget.

Afterward we went to see the house, and I perceived my Lord North and my lady shifted about to leave Mr Spencer and my lady alone so I thought I was obliged to do so too.

We left them then in some of the rooms and when we 3 had gone about we at last came into the court where the balconie is, and I saw Mr Spencer talking to my lady, in the balcony and truly for my part I did not see any passage there or any action of his but what became a very civill gentleman. I say this because I have heard that my Lord North says he kist my lady in the balcony before us all, but I protest I saw not the least of it, nor do I think by the distance I saw him keep afterward at supper, that he could have had the confidence to offer it. After this we sate down to eat some lobsters and oysters for supper. My lord often drank healths and among others Mr Spencer's and my Lady W.'s in one glass, which I remember I thought displeased her much and I did not name it so at my turne nor did she pledge it.

It was pretty late before we got back to London and we came to my Lord North's house.

In the way as we came home my Lord North spoke highly in praise of Mr Spencer's person, said he had been a traveller and was a vast schollar and for his estate it was £1500 per annum a grant from the crowne to my Lord Powis,[7] Lord Sunderland[8] and this Mr Spencer of the same summe to each of them. His paternal estate was only £600 per annum which his lady knew very [f. 2] well, for it lay just by her land in what county I forget.

---

[7] *Lord Powis*: i.e., William Herbert, Baron Powis. After the accession of James II he became the leader of the moderate Roman Catholics and later went into exile with James II.

[8] *Lord Sunderland*: Robert Spencer, Earl of Sunderland (1640-1702). He was made Lord President in 1685 and principal Secretary of State, one of the privy councillors. He sat on the High Commission when King James II revived it in July 1686. The present Robert Spencer claimed to be a 'cousin' of the earl.

I remember one passage more, remarkable. My lord got Spencer's handkerchief and he filld it with grapes and tyed it fast to the string of the glass in my Lady W.'s coach (in which my lord and I came home) and tyed it so very fast that when my lady was going into her owne coach from my Lord North's house in Leicester fields,[9] she went to untie the handkerchief seeing it not her own but could not. However she said she would send it as soon as she came home. Says my lord to Mr Spencer after my Lady W. went, *There is an opportunity for you to waite on her to fetch your hank[erchief]* - but I was told she sent it presently and all that was spoilt.

Mr Spencer offerd to have got into my lady's coach to have waited on her home, but she pusht him by the shoulder, I remember very well, and shut the coach doore, telling him that no men went in her coach with her.

After that, I think the very next day, I went to my Lady W.'s house and I heard her express so many words upon what past at Tooting as assured me she had a perfect aversion for Mr Spencer and she was very much concerned at my Lord North's carriage to her.

I went out of towne for about 5 or 6 days and at my returne I waited on her, and found that there was a very great difference between my Lord North and her. She said she would never see his face more if she could help it.

In Michaelmas Terme following, I met Spencer in Westminster Hall[10] and talking how he had been abused by my lady's brother[11] who said he had no estate etc., he told me that he beleived I had seen how kind my lady had been to him at Tooting. I said that I saw not the least likeness of it.

He said she had promist him marriage and now denies it and was gone into the country. I askt him why he would offer to say such a thing which I was sure he knew was very false. However, I said if my lady had promist she would be as good as her word, but if I might judge by what I saw I told him I ever thought she had

---

[9] *Leicester fields*: This was situated not far south of Elizabeth Wiseman's house in Soho Square, near Gerrard Street, and south of Leicester House. This is near what is now Leicester Square.

[10] *Westminster Hall*: A hall in the Palace of Westminster where the English Common Law Courts sat until the opening of the Royal Courts of Justice in the Strand in 1884. For accounts of this meeting between Thomas Chute and Robert Spencer see Documents 34 and 35.

[11] *my lady's brother*: this is Roger North. The accusation is repeated in both Documents 34 and 35.

rather an aversion than love for him. He said the day was set for their marrying. He told me the day and I askt what time he came to my Lady's house [f. 2v] that day; and after some pause he said *At five of the clock at night*. Why so late Mr Spencer? I replied, you were an indifferent lover indeed. Oh (he said) twas the way at court to marry late.

Well says I Mr Spencer you are not so madd to go to law for her, what witnesses have you? Why my Lord North and my Lady North were very good witnesses and knew all he said was very true. But however he said, if my lady's mind was chang'd he would not force her against her inclinations or words to that effect (for I took great notice of them).

I heard him speake fine things of himselfe and his family which I replied nothing to, but we parted and his resolutions I took to have been bent more to have had satisfaction of some relations who had put very great abuses upon him and his family (as he said) rather then of my lady her selfe.

Document 3
'Lady Wiseman's letter to Sir D. North Sept. 27 '86'
[in Elizabeth Wiseman's hand]

[f. 1] Deare Brother:

I thank you for the fauor of your kind vissit last night, and doe hope you gott well home and allso that my pretty godson[12] continues well after his iourny. My sister North [i.e., Lady North] you know was prevented yesterday by company so that she could haue no private conference with me about a very great concern, and therefore has doubled the vissit vpon me: for she has this night wearied me out with the discourse of that Mr Spencer I told you of; the second brother of Hanwell,[13] heyre to his mother's

---

[12] *my pretty godson*: this is Dudley North's eldest son, Dudley (1684-1715).

[13] *Hanwell*: in Oxfordshire, 3.5 miles north-west of Banbury. Spencers had lived in Hanwell and the nearby villages of Yarnton and Adderbury for several generations. In the latter part of the seventeenth century William Spencer, presumably the elder brother of Robert Spencer, the subject of these documents, and related by marriage to the Copes who were lords of the manor, lived in the manor house at Hanwell. The county records for Hanwell during the 1670s and 1680s mention also three sisters, Penelope, Margaret and Rachel.

Hanwell is near Wroxton, the seat of the late Lord Keeper, Sir Francis North, elder brother to Dudley, Elizabeth, Mountague and Roger, and it may be for this reason that Dudley North says that he knows the Spencer family, see Document 10.

fortune of £600 a yeare: and the king (within this month) has been so kind to him (vpon the account of his great relations at court) as to settle the inheritance of £1500 a yeare crown lands vpon him now in prezent: he shall be made a lord, haue what place at court he will accept of and all the kindness his relations can doe for him if he can prevaile with me to receiue his address. She has been so earnest, and vyolent with me that I could not deney giueing her a vissit to morrow night, and stay supper where I fancy this young gentleman will be. Now heareing you say you design'd to waite vpon my brother North [i.e., Charles North]: I could wish, it stood with your conveniency to come, at (or about the) houre of 6 *that you may take a view of this hobby horss*,[14] *that we may haue something to laugh at* next meeting. I haue had many things said to me by the same person, in disparagment of the other: but I am to see for my loue and buy for my mony: and 'tis not at all to be questioned, but if I fix there you'le haue good entrest at court. Pray pardon the impertinence of this, and beleive (as really it is) that my head is so addle that I scarce know what I write. My most humble seruice to all concludes me

Your most really affectionate sister and humble seruant
Kings Square[15]   Elizabeth Wyseman
Monday night 11 clock

Document 4
'Lord North's letter to Lady Wiseman 1 Oct. 1686'
[in Charles North's hand]

[Addressed: 'These to the Lady Wiseman at her house in Kings Square in So Hoe Buildings present']

[f. 1]   1st Oct[o]bre 1686
Dear Sister

Yesterday from London I was surprized with your late resolve by letter to my wife. Indeed it is late very late, now when mutuall fyres were raised almost to a flaming abroad, when geniall raptures attended only the ceremonial part for their completion and a day named for that. Were he disagreable in person, that the first addresse has informed inough the contrary. Is he faulty in witt,

---

[14] *hobby horss*: *OED* sb. 3. transf. a. a person who plays ridiculous antics, a buffoon (*Ex*. 1588–*a*.1616).
[15] *Kings square*: King's Square named after Gregory King by whom it was laid out in 1680. It was also named Soho Square.

reason, or iudgment? I am sure your own fayles you not and you know the contrary. Is his fortune to[o] small? *If he does not to the full make out what his first and last word promised reject him utterly; then he is no man of his word and shall have me his enemy.* Ay but he is vitious and is naught, would surprize you into libertyes nothing fitt in the state you are, and you cannot in sedate thoughts ever fancy such will ever make a good husband long. If his former life had been vitious, extravagant or licentious well might you then have a guesse for the future. Pray sister doe but equall justice, inquire of all that know him and if his life be hitherto untainted, lett not heats in love be misinterpreted. What will tame a mad bull? marry him. Believe me his reason and religion is too great for thoughts of that last favour[16] before publique leave. He knew it your province to deny and lesser attempts are so naturall that a cold lover never makes woman happy. But you are offred many of better estates. Doubtlesse, and if happinesse consists only in the much you might find it elswhere; what of all this? is not his [£]600 a yeare well come by? Is not the king's[17] favour as to [£]1500 a year more; certain as extraordinary. Is not so near an alliance to the favorite family[18] valuable in our day? Looke about you sister and see if such a strengthening be not good for us all.

I say no more for upon perusall of your pretious epistle I find the more agreable is to your mind. For God's sake give your body his due and your mind cannot but find it in so worthy a gentleman of an agreable age, desirable proportion, features, complexion, great in family, weighty in reason, of a smart witt and yett most sedate and sober in life and conversation, with a competent estate and that loves you passionately. Desires only you not yours. Leaves your own estate to your private disposition and menage. What would you more? I am sure also you affect[19] him, and lett me pronounce: you can only be happy in him and he with you. Be wise and consider in this your day, I am and will be in all sincerity Madam

Your truly most affectionate brother and servant
North and Grey.

---

[16] *that last favour*: i.e., sexual intercourse.
[17] *king's*: i.e., James II's.
[18] *favorite family*: i.e., the family of Robert Spencer, the Earl of Sunderland, the favourite at James II's court.
[19] *affect*: *OED vb. trans.* 2. like or love (a person) (*Ex.* 1550-1760).

Document 5
'11. Oct. 1686. Memoriall Concerning sister Wiseman'
'A Relation of what hath passed within my knowledg and observation concerning the pretences of Mr Spencer to my sister, the Lady Wiseman. 11 Oct. 1686'
[in Roger North's hand]

[f. 1] Vpon my arrivall in London together with my brother Mountague, upon Saturday the 2d Oct. 1686 at 4 in the afternoon wee went to make her a visit; when she acquainted us with an address that had bin made to her by Mr Spencer, by the procurement[20] and countenance[21] of my Lord North and his lady. And that she had seen him at his hous in Leister Feilds, and once at his hous at Tooting, she being invited to those places by him. That she did not like him and was resolved to have nothing to doe with him; and she say'd that at those places he was rude and uncivill to her, and she thought her self ill used by her brother my Lord North, for bringing her into such inconveniences; that she went to my Lady North, to declare to her that such was her resolution, and whilst she was there Mr Spencer was sent for, and was by my Lord North, and his lady put into a room to her, and she was deteined there severall hours against her will, and then he behaved himself rudely as before. And afterwards, that Lady North brought Mr Spencer to her hous, and went away and left him there, against her will and desire. And that she all along declared she would have nothing to doe, nor be concerned with him. And that she had wrote a letter to the Lord North[22] a copy of which she shewed me whereby she positively declared she would not ever entertaine any proposals relating to a match with him or to that effect. And besides she declared an abominable aversion she had to him, and to the Lord North for seducing her into so much inconvenience as his company was to her. [f. 1v] And I have observed that aversion increas in her, continually to this hour, being continually more sensible of the affonts she had received, and also being troubled with the farther pressing, and attempts of Mr Spencer, notwithstanding she used what means she could to affront him, and all that came upon his errants.

---

[20] *procurement*: OED sb. 1. arrangement, instigation, contrivance (*Ex.* 1301-1886).
[21] *countenance*: OED sb. 8. (quoting from Johnson's Dictionary) patronage; appearance of favour (*Ex.* 1576-1864).
[22] See Charles North's reply, Document 4.

The next thing remarkable was a letter which[23] a person, that I supposed was a servant of my Lord President [Sir Robert Spencer], brought directed to mee from his lordship. Upon perusall of it I found that his lordship taking notice of an address his cozen had made to my sister the Lady Wiseman, he desired that I would speak to her on his behalf, whereby he should be much oblidged. The messenger prest for an answer in writing, which I declined, finding his lordship's comand no such thing, but desired him to present my humble service to his lordship, and to say from me, that I would obey his lordship's comands as much as in me lay; and that I suppose my Lord President may understand as I did, as much as consisted with the honesty, and service to my sister. *Tantum possumus, quantum iure (vel honeste) possumus.*[24] This letter I sent away to my Lady Wiseman, for her to have due consideration of. I have seen another letter to my brother Dudly, and also to my Lord North in the same hand, and much to the same effect, but the phrase somewhat varyed.

After this Mr Spencer the elder brother, with his brother the pretender came, as upon a visit, to me in my chamber in the Temple, and my brother Mountague hapned to be present. He [i.e., the elder brother] fell upon discoursing his brother's pretensions, how well he had bin received, what favours, and at last how badly he had bin treated; he say'd that it was strang[e] after such favours, of a sudden to be so rejected, that he [f. 2] could not come to the speech of her ladyship or have his messages in any sort received, but be repulsed at the door in a positive denyall. He concluded that some persons had injured their family by reports, and he should in time know who they were. That his brother's fortune was £600 per annum and £1500 the king had given him. I asked what that was, he answered it was not yet time, or that he could not give a particular account of it. He say'd he heard that some had reported his brother's estate of £600 per annum was incumbred with 2 judgments, and a mortgage. I say'd I never heard any such thing. Then he askt if I had received a letter from my Lord Sunderland, which I agreed, and the answer I related; he ask't if I would speak etc. I say'd I could give him no other answer then I had given my Lord President, viz., that I would doe all that in me lay to obey his lordship's commands. He say'd that they must needs speake with the Lady Wiseman, to set their family right, which they perceived

---

[23] MS follows this with a deleted passage: 'Mr Spencer of Hanwell the elder brother brought'.

[24] *Tantum possumus, quantum iure (vel honeste) possumus*: (Latin) what we would do we can do only in so far as we can do it justly (or virtuously).

was traduced[25] to her, and desired but one small favour of me, which was that I would introduce them to the presence of the Lady Wiseman to have a quarter of an hour's discours with her. I refused it in totidem verbis[26] and declared for reason, that I, as the rest of my brothers, had declined to patronize, or disswade any matches with my sister, nor to intermedle with her chois which wee desired should be her owne; the rather becaus wee were under an obloquy, of endeavouring to hinder her of all matches, out of an expectation of advantage to ourselves. And wee would avoid the occasion of that; and as I remember[27] I say'd that advisers of matches run great hazzards, therefore she should choos for herself. Then they took leav, and went away, and I heard that my brother Dudley had a like visit, with somewhat more discours upon the matters aforesaid, but with no more effectuall complyance then from me.

[f. 2v] In the mean time my sister has mentioned to us the severall attempts that had bin made by the Spencers and their he and she agents, and the shifts she made to avoid them.

The next adventure was upon Sunday, the 10th October when at my sister's hous before dinner, I being playing upon the harpsicalls[28] and she singing in the room next the square, my brother the Lord North came to the door in his coach, and the boy, upon the generall orders he had received, say'd to his servant that she was not at home. So his lordship went away againe. But in the afternoon, he and Mr Spencer the pretender, came together to St Anne's church,[29] and sate the next pew but one. My sister at first sight turned from them, and I did not see her give a cast[30] that way, and she say'd afterwards, she knew nothing more of them then a single glan[c]e at first so as just to know my brother was there. After church my brother my Lord North's gentleman, came to know if she were at home, and when, but [was] answered with put offs.

---

[25] *traduced*: OED v. trans. 3. defamed, maligned, misrepresented (*Ex.* 1586-1815).

[26] *in totidem verbis*: (Latin) *literally* in so many words; briefly.

[27] In the left-hand margin MS has 'qu[ery]'.

[28] *harpsicalls*: harpsichord.

[29] *St Anne's church*: i.e., St Anne's Westminster, in Wardour Street, Soho. In *New Remarks of London* ... (1732), p. 253, St Anne's parish is described: 'The Parish was taken out of that of St Martin in the Fields, by Act of Parliament ... and finished in 1686.' The parish was divided into two liberties: Soho Square was in the upper liberty, Leicester Square and Leicester Fields (where Sir Charles North lived) were in the lower liberty.

[30] *cast*: OED sb. 6. glance (*Ex.* 1325-1768).

But that which is most materiall of all, is a visit my lord North made me at the Temple[31] this present Monday 11 October 1686 at about 9 in the morning, which I reckoned very extraordinary considering the distance between him and me. After he sate he discourst of the address, the person, the estate and the suddain chang that had bin, which must proceed from the impressions some had made, by which I understood he mean't me, but to clear the point, I assured him she had made him a positive refusall before I came to towne, and that she had wrote to his lordship or lady to that effect, a copy of which she had shewed me at my first visit to her. Then I had much adoe to perswade him that I did not come to towne the week before; and next, he affirmed that she received Spencer at her hous the Sunday following such her letter, in the evening till 11 at night, which by good luck, I could confute also, for I was with her all that afternoon, and she supt at my [f. 3] hous that night, and stay'd there so late that it was ten before she could gett home. And I told him in short I found her in an absolute aversion to Mr Spencer's pretences,[32] which had continued and increased and I veryly beleeved was implacable. And I thought Mr Spencer being a gentleman and finding that the case was so, he ought to rest satisfied, and not give her any more trouble. He say'd that if wee were not in towne brother Dudley was, and he must be the occasion of her great chang; I say'd he, I supposed, would answer for himself. Then his lordship say'd that this buissnes must not rest here, it would be ill for her, if she did not adhere to her first intentions, and marry Mr Spencer. He had hinted in his letter to her,[33] which he supposed I had seen that she would be happy in no other man but Mr Spencer, and he took it [she] could not have any other, so farr had it proceded. This made me, out of curiosity to know what was pretended,[34] ask what had bin done that should make him and Mr Spencer speak of favours, and such procedings. He say'd he took it that they had bin as good as married, or as it were contracted; (in his doubdtfull hesitating way of speaking in nice concernes). For she gave him her hand, and he put it into Mr Spencer's, and ask't her if she consented to be his wife, or to that porpose, and that she was silent. Then he asked her if her silence should taken for consent, and she still was silent,

---

[31] *the Temple*: i.e., the Middle Temple of which Roger North was a bencher and where he had his office.
[32] *pretences*: OED sb. 3. obs. expressed aims, purposes, designs (*Ex*. 1526-1783).
[33] See Document 4.
[34] *pretended*: OED v. 7. put forward as an assertion or statement; alleged (*Ex*. 1639-1781).

and that this he would averr, and that imediately a day was appointed, Thursday morning as I remember. Then I told him that he ought in honour to protect his sister from such pretences[35] as these were, and not foment them as I perceived he did. He answered, true if she had not consented, but now it is too far gon, and it must not stop here, and thought himself bound to see right done, and he should prosecute as farr as he might, and he spoke much in a way of admonition that if this match did not succeed, it would be wors for us, meaning as I understood him, with relation to our stations in the king's service, and the Earl of Sunderland's power, and say'd that my brother Dudley and I should hear of it from the highest, and bid us Look too't, severall times. I say'd I would act [f. 3v] as an honest man, be the event what it would. I mentioned the insolent and rude behaviour that I had heard my sister complain of Mr Spencer, and him with detestation; what said he, love tricks? can she thinck ever to be happy in a formall lover? and took notice of his letter,[36] in answer to hers whereby she signified her refusall, that he had answered that objection there, and all others that could be pretended.[37] And he say'd iff he could but have a litle discours with her in our presence he did not doubdt but to convince her of her mistake, and bring her to perfect amity with Mr Spencer againe, and desired that I would appoint a time, to meet; I sayd I could not appoint for my brothers but would speak with them, and then send to his lordship. Then he would himself goe to brother Dudley and make the appointment. He spoke of the bad usage he had had from her, denying her se'f, when she was within, and saying she was to goe to the park, and did not, etc. I say'd that she had a positive resolution to admitt no visit or approach to her, from Mr Spencer or any that came on his account, as she knew he did, therefore he must not take it ill, for it is the buissness onely that she rejects. Amongst his discours of the favours Mr Spencer had received, he say'd that when they were together in the room, so long, she might have come out if she had pleased, no body held the door; and if the door were fast how did she come out at last. And when shee came out she cry'd, Fy fy Mr Spencer. So that she was willingly in his company, and not much offended at what was done there; and what that might be for saying, Fy fy, sufficiently declared. Upon this he departed saying he would at 4 goe to brother Dudley to make an appointment. Which

---

[35] *pretences*: OED sb. see note 32, above.
[36] See Document 4.
[37] *pretended*: OED v. I. 2. brought forward (*Ex. c.* 1450-1690).

14 LIFE INTO STORY

is the substance of what past be[t]wixt us, to the best of my recollection.

I must not forget what I heard my sister declare, that his lordship [i.e., Charles North], before his going out of towne, came to her and desired she would give him some satisfaction in this affair, he did not press her to marry but if she would give him some litle wrighting or contract under her hand, it would be extreamly to his content and satisfaction.

Document 6
'Lord North's letter to Lady Wiseman 13 October 1686'
[in Charles North's hand]

[Addressed: 'For the Lady Wiseman']
[f. 1] Sister,
Consider what you have done and what you deserve if so worthy a servant dies upon your damnd usage of him. If there be any honour or charity left send some one or other. Enquire whither he be in reality drawing on[38] or dissembles. I say not but he may recover but so it is a high feavour he labours under. Has sent for Doctour Tenison.[39] His councill is needfull to him. If his honour and conscience had not stood in his light these pangs had never been his lott. Farewell and be wiser then you have been. Your younger brothers lead you by the nose, making you forswear what you love. Vengeance will follow such barbarisme.
    Octbre 13th.
    North and Grey.
His lodging is over against Bedford house.[40] Inquire after him if all humanity has not left you.

---

[38] *drawing on*: OED v. 86. e. obs.: drawing near to death (*Ex.* 1555-1577).
[39] *Doctour Tenison*: i.e., Thomas Tenison (1636-1715), later Archbishop of Canterbury. He was at Cambridge University from 1653 to 1657 and might have known Charles North then. He was appointed to St Martin-in-the-Fields in 1680 and in 1686 also to St James's Piccadilly.
[40] *Bedford house*: in the Strand, Westminster, in the early seventeenth century the residence of the Russell family.

Document 7
'Letter to sister Wiseman about Sir Jo. Thorold 14 Oct. 1686'
[in Roger North's hand]

[f. 1] Dearest Bess,

I have had an account of Sir John's [i.e. Sir John Thorold's] estate of which brother Dudley will give a more particular account and I find nothing but what is very landed[41] and open, as to the title and incumbrances. Now it will be necessary for you to consider and determine what termes you will require. I thinck a rent charg upon his whole estate, will be the best joynture, because the widdow[42] claimes a dower, which I cannot ensure against, but there is probable matter to barr it. If that prevailes no part can be secured clear from it to you. And if they are not willing to incumber the estate with so great a charg as you may reasonably expect for a joynture, then you may have some of your owne fortune set apart, for such porposes, as you shall agree upon. Brothers will discors more largly. That knight is now with me, and 2 brothers [i.e., Dudley and Mountague North]. I found this way to bring them to acquaintance, and remember I begin to be out of your dett, being desirous ever to remain in your esteem for

14 Oct   the most etc., Roger North.
1686.

Document 8
'Message from Sir Jo. Thorold 16 Oct. 1686'
[in Roger North's hand]

[f. 1] Mr Gipps Sir John Thorold's Agent, came to me about 6, this present Saturday 16 Oct. 1686, to acquaint me, that Sir Jo. had heard from some of his relations, (unkles I think he mentioned) in the country, who understanding that he was about to alter his condition, had wrote to him, to desire that he would forbear till they came to towne, which would be about a fortnight hence, to the end they might consult with, and advise him in so weighty a matter. And that he was desirous to comply with their request, the

---

[41] *landed*: OED a. 1. possessed of land; in this context, with the meaning of well possessed and with clear title.

[42] *the widdow*: Sir John Thorold's mother, Grissill Ray (or Wray). Details of the Thorold family and their estates are found among the papers of Dr Thomas North at Rougham Hall, Norfolk. They were prepared by Roger North in anticipation of a settlement for his sister's proposed marriage.

rather that he might have the benefit of their assistance in the treaty; and this he informed mee supposing I would acquaint the Lady W. with it, so that she might not thinck much, if Sir J. did not, in that time, wait upon her as he ought and it may be she might expect from one in his pretences.[43] I say'd I should see her tomorrow, and would acquaint her, and did thinck it most just that one in his case should have the advice of his freinds. And I farther ask't him some questions concerning the wills in the family. He told me that Sir William upon whome the setlement was made dyed in his father's life time, and had not power to charg the estate. Sir William the eldest son of Anthony, made no will but dy'd an infant. Sir Ant. the brother of Sir William, this gentleman's elder brother, made no will.[44] I insisted to see what wills were whether material or not. I desired also that if there were any farther progress, that he would prepare the evidence of the rest of Sir John's title, which is not in the setlement, for our satisfaction, all which he sayd he would doe. And in particular Mr Gipps desired I would not proceed in making any draught, till I heard farther. I say'd I had began none, nor would till I heard from my sister what she expected, and had agreed and then I would serve her the best I could.

Document 9
'Memorandum of Sir John Thorold's visit. 19 Oct. 1686.'
[in Roger North's hand]

[f. 1] Vpon the 19th Oct. 1686 Sir Jo. Thorold came to my chamber soon after 3 in the afternoon, and being sate, began to relate the message he had received from one Mr Spencer. He say'd that the person was very civil, and acquainted him, that Mr Spencer hearing he had made an address to the Lady Wiseman thought fit

---

[43]*in his pretences*: pretence, *OED* sb. 3. *obs.* purpose, design (*Ex.* 1526-1783). The *OED* gives no use in the plural nor the phrase 'in pretences'. The meaning here is 'with his purposes'.

[44]*He told me ... made no will*: The 'Sir William upon whom the settlement was made' was uncle of Sir John and the eldest son. He married Elizabeth, daughter of Sir Robert Carr, in 1648 and 'the setlement' was made at the time of that marriage. He died without issue. The second Sir William mentioned was Sir John's eldest brother who died in infancy. The 'Sir Ant. the brother of Sir William' was the brother of the Sir William who died in infancy, the second son of the family and Sir John's elder brother. He married in 1683 Anna Maria, daughter of Sir Thomas Harrington. The present Sir John Thorold was the third son of Anthony Thorold and Grissill Ray.

to send him to him, to let him know that that lady was his wife before God, and he must have her; for they were contracted, and he had good wittnesses to prove it, and intended to prosecute at law for her; therefore he must have a care how he visited her. Sir John say'd that his answer was, that for visiting the Lady Wiseman or not visiting her, he should not give Mr Spencer nor any an account. And he should be alwais ready to justifie his actions as became him. And as for the rest he knew not why Mr Spencer should trouble himself to send to him, and might proceed as he pleased. He say'd farther that the gentleman told him that Mr Spencer's wittnesses were very good, and substantiall, and that he was 4 hours alone with the lady; and, as I remember, that his witnesses heard what past betwixt them. I say'd that I thought my sister's honnour above his calumny, or the calumny of any els, and I beleev'd she as she had reason, did despise that, and the authors and abbettors of it. And that she and also wee would consider what was fitt to be done, and act accordingly. And I was of opinion that to take notice of such lys, would give them more credit then they deserved, or would otherwise have. After this he say'd that he hoped he might be excused in not proceeding any farther in the affair of the Lady Wiseman seeing it was so confidently pretended[45] that she was contracted, and that there were substantiall wittnesses; and the event of law-suits was not so certein but sometimes sentences were otherwise then they ought to be and he did not know how farr and beleeved it probable, that the cunning of these disigners may have bin too hard for the lady, who neither had reason to suspect any such designe nor knew the critiscisme of such points, and that she may possibly be drawne into what she cannot extricate herself from; and it could not be expected he should be concerned in the [f. 1v] consequence of such questions, and in short flatly discharged himself of his farther prosecuting any pretences[46] of marrying with the lady. All that I sayd was that God forbid but he should have full liberty to act according to his owne judgment, as others had. He say'd he was fully sensible of the ill treatment the lady had had, and of the falsness of these suggestions; he presented his service to the lady, and I to his sisters, and so he departed in a full refusall of farther treaty, as I understood him.

---

[45]*pretended*: *OED v.* I. 7. alleged (*Ex.* 1610-1839).
[46]*pretences*: *OED sb.* 3. *obs.* expressed aims, intentions (*Ex.* 1526-1783).

18 LIFE INTO STORY

Document 10
'Narrative of Sir D. North relating to the Lady Wiseman 22 October 1686'
[in Dudley North's hand]

[f. 1] On Friday the 17 Sept., I returned to London from where I had been absent above 6 weekes. The Sunday following I went with my wife to visit my sister Wiseman, who met my sister North. On Tewsday morning following I received a letter from my sister Wiseman intimating that my sister North had been againe with her and proposed a match with one Mr Spencer and had told her great things of him for her, and to the opinion she then had of him I refer to the letter.[47] In the said letter she said that she had promised to goe that evening to my brother North's and supp there when she should see him and desired mee, having heard mee say that I intended my brother a visit, to fall in as it were accidentaly and meet her there. Accordingly between 6 and 7 I went thither, but no body was at home but my sister North with whom I discoursed a good while of indifferent matters. At last discoursing of my sister Wiseman my sister North told mee that she had provided her a husband a most extraordinary person great in fauour at court, of £600 per annum paternall estate and one that the king had lately given [£]1500 per annum, crowne lands to, but told mee not his name. While wee were discoursing my sister came in, when my sister North went over the whole story againe with mighty encomiums on the man and his owne and freinds' great power at court that he could doe what he would and in her discourse threatned those that should oppose the match,[48] [f. 1v] but did not name the person, nor did I ask. But my sister Wiseman spake out and said she beleived I knew the man and said it was a yonger son[49] to Mr Spencer of Hanwell by Wroxton. I said I had neuer seene him nor did not know that there was such a man, but I had ben at Hanwell and been obliged to the family there, when my sister North replyed that tho he was a younger brother yet he had an elder brother's fortune, and so forth etc. After I had continued a good while there much longer then course of a common visit, I began to take my leave when my sister North

---

[47] This letter does not survive. It is clear from Document 3, Elizabeth's first surviving letter in the series, that she had already informed her brother Dudley about Mr Spencer.
[48] MS follows this with a deleted passage: 'after I had continued a good while there much longer then the course of common visit I began to take my leave'.
[49] Preceded in MS by 'brother', deleted.

once faintly asked why I would goe, but my sister Wiseman pressed my stay. But being pretty late I came away. I saw not my sister Wiseman nor heard anything from her till Thursday following when going with my wife to visit her she gave us an account of all that had passed at my brother North's house and att Tooting, and was angry that I left her aloane at my Lord North's *and said that tho she promised to goe to Tooting yet intended it not and sent to excuse it in the morning but my sister North would admit of noe excuse nor denyall but said if she would not goe with them they would come and bee with her all day, whereupon she resolved to goe but desired my cozen Thomas Chute who came to see her to goe with her not caring to be aloane with them. She complained very much at the great rudenesses of Mr Spencer both times but most espetialy at Tooting and in the coach coming from thence, she very much exclaimed* against Mr Spencer and my brother and sister North and said she would have nothing to doe with them euer any more. [f. 2] I saw not my sister nor heard any more from her till Saturday when she came to my house and told mee (complaining) of the ill vsage she had met with at my brother North's the day before and said[50] that she went thither only to tell them plainly and seriously that she would not haue Mr Spencer on any account what euer and that they kept her there perforce and sent for Mr Spencer and put them into a roome together and shutt the doores where Mr Spencer kept her, not suffering her to come to the doore, for seuerall howres. She said she thought my brother and sister were mad and would marry her to that man perforce whom she detested and would be torne to peices before she would come in his company againe. While she was at my house my sister North came in also to giue my wife a visit, and wee were all together for the time she stayed which was not long, and I doe not remember that there was any discouse at all passed concerning Mr Spencer in publick but my sister North often whispered with my sister Wiseman, which after my sister North was gon she told us was to haue her goe to her house. But my sister Wiseman (as she told us) answered that she had buissnesse in the citty and could nott. She said also that she beleiued she was dogged to my house for she had denyed her selfe, but a little before when my sister North and Mr Spencer came to her house. She stayed a good while before she went home on purpose to auoid being troubled with them, which she often declared she could not endure. After this not hearing from my sister in some dayes, I

---

[50] MS follows this with a deleted passage: 'shee thought my brother and sister North were both mad and ... they kept her'.

thinke Wednesday I went to giue her a uisit but she was not att home, coming at the same time to my house so I missed her, but at my returne I heard [f. 2v] from my wife what had happened the Sunday before and how my sister North and Mr Spencer got into her house against her will and stayed there some time together, when my sister North went away and left Mr Spencer aloane with her, saying she had brought him there but would not carry him away againe but leaue him there. Mr Spencer stayd some howres but she said she made her man servant and her maid sit in the next roome and the dores open all the while, which Mr Spencer was angry at. This I had by relation from my wife, but all confirmed by my sister the next time I saw her which I doe not punctualy remember when it was but I thinke itt was the next day. The Saturday following my brothers came to towne.

Not long after I received a letter from my Lord Sunderland by a gentleman that I supposed was one of his lordship's family. The purport of it only was that I should assist his kindsman in his adresses to my sister. The gentleman that brought the letter desired to haue my answer, to whom I replyed that I thought the letter needed none[,] that I had a great honor for my Lord Sunderland as I ought[,] and that I desired him to assure his lordship that that letter should haue its due weight. Soone after my brother Mountagu going to my sister Wiseman carried my Lord Sunderland's letter to her which I did that she might see and understand my lord's plans in behalfe of his kindsman. Not long after, I received a visit from Mr Spencer the elder brother whom I had knowne at Hanwell and his brother who made addresses to my sister. They asked mee if I had received a letter from my Lord Sunderland. I told them I had and the purport of it [f. 3] and the answer I had made to it. They complained to mee that they feared that somebody had don it officious to my sister, and traduced their family for whereas Mr Spencer had been kindly receiued by her and had favours from her, now she would not so much as admit him or any of them or theire sister or any body from them to see her or deliuer a message, which they woundred mightyly at and said could not proceed but from lyes told of them and their relations. Now they desired of mee that I would doe them the fauour to preuaile with my sister that they might but once be admitted to her presence to justifie themselues and their family, to which I answered that I should be glad if I could doe them any seruice, as well in obedience to my Lord Sunderland's commands as for their owne sakes, but I would not undertake to carry them without my sister's leaue, least her doores might be shutt against me as they had been against them. And I further told them that I uery much wondred to hear them talke of kindnesses and fauours from my sister which they seemed to declare to haue been very extraordinary and I desired Mr Spencer to acquaint me how and of what nature those fauours were, to which Mr Spencer replyed Nothing, but what was very ciuell and might haue passed before all the world, but that she receiued his adresses kindly and willingly which I told him I wondered very much at, being she had from the very beginning declared the contrary to mee and was so farr from acknowledg[ing] any kindness for him that to mee she had alwayes expressed the contrary, and that I should and might sweare if cal[l]ed upon.

[f. 3v] This passed on a Thur[s]day. I told them I was not sure to haue oportunity to see my sister before Sunday and then I should certainly be with her, and if they would lett me know where they lodged, if my sister would give me leave to bring them to her house, I would willingly waite upon them to doo it. I went next day to my sister but she would not admit [me]. Soone after caling att my brother Roger's chambers as I was going to the treasury I understood my brother North had been there and would be with mee that after noone about the same bussinesse, on which I sent my boye to his house to acquaint him of the nessessity of my attending the treasury but that at my returne from thence I would waite upon him, and accordingly did, but found only Mr Spencer and my sister North. But soone after my brother North came in, I acquainted Mr Spencer that I had been with my sister the day after he had been at my house but she absolutely refused to see him. They admired much what might be the reason of this (as they said) so great change in her. I said I could giue no account of it but must declare that to mee all along from the very beginning she had professed the contrary and that excepting the 2 first times she had been in his company perforce and not willingly; and asking what the extraordinary fauours were that were so much talked of, my brother North replyed that she had kissed him publickly in the balcony at Tooting in the sight of his footmen to which Mr Spencer replyed Noe she did not kisse him, but he indeed kissed her in the belcony there. They insisted very much that I would endeauour that my sister would admitt them to speake [f. 4] with them. I said I could promise nothing but I would waite upon her and know her pleasure and shou[l]d be well pleased that she would doo it. My brother and sister North had a great deale of extrauagant discourse importing threats to them that should crosse this match and said that not only my Lord Sunderland but the king also concerned himselfe therein. My brother North seemed extraordinaryly concerned that my sister Wiseman should not only deny herselfe to Mr Spencer but to him allso when he knew she was at home which he thought uery unreasonable and extraordinary he being the head of our family. Next day I went to my sister in company with brother M[ountague] and acquainted her with all that had passed, but found her possitiuely determined neuer to see Mr Spencer any more, but she said if my brother and sister North would give themselues the trouble to come to her house any time when wee were there she would see them and acquaint them with the reasons she had for what she had don. With this message immediately my brother M. and I went to my Lord North, where inquiring for my brother wee were carried upstaires where my sister came to us presently and my brother not long after, when [I] told them what my sister Wiseman had said, that is that she would neuer see Mr Spencer againe but if my brother and sister North would come to her house when wee were there, she would see them and tell them her reasons etc. To which my brother North replyed, Not he; if she would not admitt Mr Spencer he would not goe, nor neuer come in her dores againe, and further said that what had passed betweene them if insisted upon he [f. 4v] beleiued would amount to a contract, but he beleued it would not be insisted upon. Hee also pointing to a couch and a chair said, That couch and that chair knows what passed betwixt them, and a great deale of such stuff. Wee made but a shorte visit, not sitting downe but came away.

And this to the best of my remembrance is what passed in this affair wherein I was anywayes concerned.
   Wrote the 22 October 1686

Document 11
'Copy of a letter to Sir G. Weneev, about Sr. Wiseman' no date [most in Dudley North's hand]

[f. 1] Wee have undertaken to write you this letter in joynt that it might haue the weight it requires, being in a very important case wherin no lesse then the honor of our whole family is concerned, *and wee hope and doubt not but you will in such a case be assisting to us.*
   And wee presume that wee may depend on you for the assistance of a brother.
   Our sister Wiseman liuing aloane by hirselfe has for some time been the aime of all the towne fopps, her estate being the bait that many of them have swallowed in immagination for a great while,

and this is now growne to that height occasioned by her owne too great want of experience and ...[51] carriage of some, who least ought to haue don[e] it, that wee have thought it absolutely nessessary for her that she remoue suddainly out of London and for some time, in which resolution wee know no better place for her to retire to then Brettnam,[52] which considering your *worth and* relation to her *and authority esteemed in the country* wee thought for the best ...[53] place.[54] She intends to sett outt on Thursday morning and in her company comes our M.N. to whom and herself wee referr you for the particular occasion that requires this which you will understand from them att large. Wee only thought fitt to let you have [f. 1v] this account before hand that you might nott be unprouided for her reception. You know uery well that she is a lady of worth[55] and will not suffer you to be at any charge for her which she will not thorougly recompence.[56] Wee are perfect participants with her in this affair and shall acknowledg all your kindness to her as done in farr greater proportion to
D.N. M.N. R.N.

Document 12
'The Lady Wiseman's relation concerning Mr Spencer. Oct. [1686]'[57]
[in Elizabeth Wiseman's hand]

[f. 1] The first time I saw Mr Robert Spencer, he came to make me a vissit from (as was pretended[58]) his relations in Oxfordshire, and I received him, there being an other gentlewoman in company with me. After a short vissit he took leaue. At this first enterview I like'd him so ill that I charg'd my servant as he went out, to take speciall notice of his face and be sure, never to lett him come within my doors any more, and accordingly they did refuse him severall times. One after noon about one aclock my Ladie North

---

[51] The rest of the line is unreadable since folding of the page has torn the paper.
[52] *Brettnam*: i.e., Brettenham, in Suffolk, the home of Sir George Wenyeve and his wife Christina, Elizabeth Wiseman's sister.
[53] The paper is torn on the fold making the rest of the line illegible.
[54] MS follows with 'to <retyre to>'.
[55] *of worth*: OED worth *sb*. 5. position or standing in respect of property (*Ex*. 1592-1812); hence, 'a lady of means'.
[56] Roger North's hand completes the letter.
[57] MS has 1678.
[58] *pretended*: OED v. 6. put forward as a reason or excuse; used as a pretext (*Ex*. 1456-1776).

sent to desire me to be within at 4, because she would speake with me about bussiness. I returned answere I would waite her pleasure at that time. A little before she comes, and tells me her lord design'd to be with me, and bring a gentleman which she was sure I could not disaproue of: great in birth, fortune etc., not nameing the person. Not long after they came, to my great amazemant that he which I had so often refus'd and disalow'd should be brought by so neere a relation, who I was sure knew as little of him as myselfe. I entertain'd them with as much coldness as 'twas possible, which was perceiu'd by other company then present and his lordship chid me for it as I waited vpon his ladie to the coach. Not long after the Ladie North came again, and wondred exstreamly at my cold reception of so worthy a gentleman as Mr S. was and mentiond what estate she was enform'd he had and affirm'd it of her own knowlidg. She told me I sate mumping[59] by the fyreside and would neuer be well till I came abroad, and desir'd me to come and eate a bitt with them at supper the next day. I answer'd I was affraid Spencer would be there; Tis no matter said she, You must see for your loue and buy for your mony, and if you dislik'd there was no harme done. I went and found accordingly S. there and before supper they took an occasion to goe out of the room, and leave us a lone together. Vpon which he began to make a very ensignificant[60] idle adress which I repuls't a[s] much as I could, and told him my dislike to him. Before supper was done I being ill with my cold, she[61] exstracted a promise from me to take the ayre of Tooting the next day and see if it would be any better, and said no body would be there but their selues. I fearing Spencer vpon second thoughts, after I gott home, resolu'd to excuse it the next morning which I did but she would take no denighall, and affirm'd her selfe to be exstreamly ill allso, and did not question but the ayre would doe us both good. When I came to her house in Leysterfields attended by cosen Thomas Chute, there according to my fears found S. who she told me had been so full of greife for my ill usiage of him the night before that he had not slept a wink, nor eate a bit of meat since. We went our iourn'y, and he walk't with me, together with the rest of the company in the garden, where he said many nonsencicall things of his passions for me as

---

[59] *mumping*: OED ppl. a. assuming a miserable aspect of countenance (*Ex.* 1594-1869).
[60] *ensignificant*: = *insignificant* OED a. 2. without weight or force (*Ex.* 1627-a. 1735).
[61] Elizabeth Wiseman puts the passage from 'she' to 'second thoughts' in parentheses.

is common in those cases: and vou'd my vnkindness would kill him. I told him all the sattisfaction I would giue him was I would consider of it, but his roughness was so odious, and displeaseing to me that I would never haue him. My Lord North would often bid me make no long bussines of it, I told him No: more I would not, with that person I [designed to marry][62] which was not Spencer and did assure him I would never marry any [person] contrary to my mind to please any particular person: his answere was God forbid I should. Next day (or day after) I went to his house to lett him know my aversion [and] resolution never to haue to doe with him or come .... once in the house I asked the porter whether my Lord N. [were at home] [f. 1v] vpon which I entre'd the house little dreaming of the treachery was design'd. As soon as I had told my brother my mind I would haue gone a way, but meeting my sister she desir'd me, being she was alone, to sitt down in the drawingroom with her which I did, and had not sate long but in comes Sp. With that I was exstreamly concern'd and said I would not stay and was mighty averss to be in his company, but they constrained me and my sister riz vp and said this was an vnusiall coyness and Mr S. must gett me into better humour, and with that went out of the room, her husband following, and clap't the door to, after them. There was I tormented with this man's flames and nonsense till it grew dusky, notwithstanding I beg'd of him and us'd all the means I could for my releasement, and would haue gone often to open the door, but he was so rude as not to suffer me, tho I entreated him and was really engaged to Mistris Foynes vpon bussiness, but all the arguments I could use did not moue him to the civillity I exspected from one that boasted so much of his gentillity. Mrs Foynes sent once or twice to know if I would come to her, but they never aquainted me with it. When I came out of the room (which I did by force after candles were light else where) Lord North came to me and catching hold of my hand clap't it to Mr Spencer's and said Come, come, make a quick bussiness of it and kiss her vpon that account, which I was so mad at, that I flang from him down stayrs, and cannot remember who putt me in the coach: but said as I stept in, I would never come more there whilst I had breath, and ordred my coach to goe to Mistris Fyne's where they were in an amaze at the trouble they saw me in and beg'd of me to vend[63] my passion that I might not burst.

---

[62] From here to the foot of the page the paper is torn and the text can be only partially pieced together. The last line of text on the page is almost completely lost.

[63] *vend*:= *vent*.

And endeed it was so very great, at the ill treatment I had received from so nere relations that 'twas impossible for me to conceale it. When I came home my servants were in as great a consternation at it, being a sufficient[64] time before I could recouer my selfe, so as to say where I had been: but after ordred them vpon pain of my displeasure not to lett Lady North nor her associates in at my doors. On Sunday after diner comes the Lord North with a desire to speake with me only two or 3 words which were in efect, that he was goeing to Cattledge[65] the next day; and that he would desire for his sattisfaction that I would show some kindness to Mr Spencer by way of contract or some such thing which putt me into so great a passion that I declar'd my selfe again, and again, with utter detestation of him and that I hated him of all men liueing and would never have him whilst I had breath. Not withstanding this he pressed my supping with them, and brought his wife and Spencer to the church where I was and would haue trapan'd[66] me from thence - She and Sp.[67] came to my house and that Sunday eve, my seruants told the messenger I was not within he [tear in the page] ... and a competent time after Spencer, and the Lady North came to the .... soon as the seruant opened it rush't in and I being then alone... to ... to them ... carry them vp stayres. The Lady North had [f. 2] sate long, but a seruant of hers (which I presume was so ordred before she got in) came and pretended his lord had sent to desire my Ladie North to come home. With that she riz vp and said Mr Spencer, I'le leaue you here. No but you shall not said I. But I will said she and with that flung down stayres and Spencer held me from following. So I walk't about the room and he pulling of me to sitt, which vpon condition of his civillity, the doors being open and my man and maid at them, I did, and there he stay'd discoursing after the same rate of impertinence he vs'd to doe, and I treated him with the same languish:[68] I never would haue him whilst I had breath, and told him if he would, I would haue all my seruants to beare wittness. So he went a way mightylie dissattisfied, and I told him he should never come within my house again, nor would I ever see him if I could avoy'd it. I slept

---

[64] *sufficient*: the OED meanings for this do not quite give the implied sense of 'a considerable time'.

[65] *Cattledge*: also Kirtling, in Suffolk, the home of Charles Lord North and Grey.

[66] *trapan'd*: OED v. trans. 2. (alternative spelling of trepanned) lured, inveigled (*Ex. a.* 1661-1838).

[67] This is followed in MS by '<after (Lord North out of town)>'.

[68] *languish*: OED sb. 1. the state of languishing; languor. But cf. Document 36 where she uses it to mean 'language'. This might be the meaning here.

not a wink that night with vexation at the ill uvsiage I had received from them both abroad and at home, and resolu'd to write my possitiue resolution to the Ladie North:
   [at the foot of this page are 6 lines of text, torn and thus
   incomplete: they may belong at the foot of f. 1v:]
whereas they say a day was sett when Lady North and Spencer, were saying Thursday was a very good day to marry in, and ask't me if it was ... my answere was all God almightys days were good and nam'd severall other dayes of the week. She told me Mr ... his pocket to be ready ... I never would and his ... [rest of the page torn off].

Documents 13 and 14
'Copy of our first letter to Sister Wiseman at Brettenham, [27] Oct. 1686.'
[in Dudley North's hand: Document 14 is a copy of this in Roger North's hand]

[f. 1] Dear Sister[69]

The inclosed were sent to us to convey to you which we thought fit to open not knowing but they might conteine some what in relation to your affairs at present wherin our endeavours or thoughts might possibly be of some seruice to you. The verses inclosed wee haue more then probable suspition were composed under the shepheards[70] and they are presented to you by way of apologie for that worthy person[71] whose martir at present you are, to the end you may not take it ill to be soe treated living when the dead have no better measure. We haue not yet had any particulars of discouery concerning the proceedings of[72] Mr S., butt expect shortly to have by meanes of your company to Tooting[73] and some

---

[69] *Dear Sister*: Roger North writes 'Dearest Bess' in Document 14.
[70] *composed under the shepheards*: perhaps a satiric reference to the enclosed letters' pretensions to literary love pastoral.
[71] *that worthy person*: Is this Sir John Thorold who had recently withdrawn his offer of marriage to Elizabeth? See Document 9. Or does Dudley North suggest that Thorold composed the verses about Spencer? But a later reference to the verses' having been distributed to both the friends and enemies of the late Lord Keeper suggests that 'that worthy person' might be a sarcastic reference to Spencer. See also Elizabeth's reply, Document 15.
[72] *of*: Roger North (in Document 14) has 'intended by'.
[73] *company to Tooting*: This is a reference to Thomas Chute who accompanied the party to Tooting; see Document 2.

others of his relations[74] who are now in towne. Thus far we have heard that Mr S.'s relations say he intends to seize [you] wherever he meets you, which is the most probable game he has left, for I doe not see that he can haue any incouragement either at law or from your inclinations and there are some of his name but of a bigger family not a little famous for violence and extravagance who would assist in any desperate undertaking. If wee find there is a persistence in the pretence of contract it will be nessessary to comence a suit in the Exchequer Court on your behalfe to be legaly discharged from it which is cal[l]ed a iactitation or bayling[75] of marriage. Such a pretence being once a foot no woman can treat in order to a match either with honor or saf[e]ty. As for the first, the opinion of the world is accordingly and with reason for none can know before the law declares whether there be truth in it or not, and for the other a suit may be comenced after marriage and children etc., and preuayling, as many times wrong doth, the consequence is divorse, bastardy and what not, to all which inconveniencyes a match is exposed. This wee have in thoughts but not to be put in execution till farther information, consideration and advice. I forgot to tell you that the verses I mentioned before were sent[76] by the penny post not only to us but to all that eminently either loued or hated the late Lord Keeper[77] that pleasure or vexation might accordingly take place. Wee doo

---

[74] Roger North (in Document 14) adds 'out of Essex'.

[75] *bayling*: Roger North (in Document 14) has 'boasting'. In both volumes of the extant manuscript version of Roger North's *Life of Dudley North* (British Library MSS Additional 32512 and 32513) North mentions the suit *pro jactitatione maritagii*: 'this Spencer was brought on and countenanced by this elder brother [i.e., Charles North], and was so insolent to pretend a contract, which afterwards was damned in a suit pro jactitatione maritagii ...' (Add. 32512, f. 153.) The other version of this matter has 'he [i.e., Spencer] had the insolence to pretend a contract which was afterwards damned by sentence in a caus thought fitt to be prosecuted, de iactitatione maritagii ...' (Add. 32513, f. 122v.). In the same passage North mentions the family's fear of the possibility of Spencer's taking action in the High Commission: 'At this time the High Comission Court was on foot, which was terrible to many under matrimoniall claimes, and Lord Sunderland, with his freind the Lord Jeffress, ruled the roast there. And Sir D. North apprehended most of all a citation *in causa contractus* from them. And somewhat came to his ear that gave him caus to suspect it ...'

It is unlikely that a case for iactitation of marriage would have been conducted in the Court of the Exchequer since most such cases were prosecuted in the Court of the Arches, the court dealing with ecclesiastical matters. It seems that the case was, indeed, pursued in the Court of the Arches, see Documents 53 and 54.

[76] Roger North (in Document 14) adds 'about'.

[77] *the late Lord Keeper*: This is a reference to their brother, Sir Francis North, who had died in 1685.

not hear yet that either the lords or gentlemen are yett gon out of towne. You see what an abominable wicked world wee liue in[78] of which you are now a suffering witnesse, and as I beleiue you could not haue immagined, that what you now know was possible so scarce any that hear it related will give credit [f. 1v] butt thinke that the story is agrauated out of malice. The falsnesse of humans is such that none who are not approued by long and great tryals are fitt to be trusted in affaires of great moment especialy where vallue and interest takes place. On the other side it is direct madnesse to trust whereeuer one instance of falsnesse has been found, and there is no better or surer rule of conduct in the world, then that a good thing from a bad hand is to be refused. In transacting with strangers or people untryed the only measure of fidelity is the truth and reality[79] of the subject matter and not att all the countenances or speeches of the persons for it is to be expected that man and womankind are all interested and cunning and designe accordingly for their owne or freinds aduantage tho they discouer it not; therefore if any such appeares[,] that must be esteemed the motiue of pretended[80] freindship, and there is no more to be considered then whether it be reasonable that such aduances should be for your sake or not or for any other end and what is reasonable in the persons you deal with construes what is said and not the import of words. For false people say the same things that become the true and honest concluding that other language is not for the purpose. Therefore new freindships are most dangerous, and the more superlatiuely violent the more suspitious, because reason comes not to that height. Wee doubt not but that you are uery well at Brettenham and certainly safe and at ease, which this towne will not permit at present, and no place of retirement but to relations would passe muster, in the censure of the medling sex, nor would any indifferent place be secure from the insults and persecutions of villaines, who I hope will not haue the impudence to follow you where you are there being one that knows how to deale with them and hath experience enough to preuent all inconueniences to you. In the meane time you must keep a good hart and passe the time with as much indifference[81] and complacence[82] as may be, being kind and respectfull to all, obliging

---

[78] *live in*: Roger North (Document 14) has 'have'.
[79] *reality*: OED sb. 1. c. correspondence to fact; truth (*Ex.* 1793).
[80] *pretended*: OED v. I. 2. proffered (*Ex. c.* 1450-1690).
[81] *indifference*: OED sb. 2. absence of feeling for or against; *esp.* absence of care for or about a person or thing (*Ex.* 1659-1848).
[82] *complacence* : OED sb. 2. b. pleasantness of temper or mien (*Ex.* 1767).

to the little ones, in particular keeping your grauity and not being
too free and open in discourse, and alwayes in what is said
consider not the opinion you haue but the opinion others with
whom you conuerse should have, for it is not truth and integrity
but appeareance and aprehension that makes caracters.[83] The
towne is so siuile as to want you married almost uniuersaly. Lady
Betty Brabazon is married to Sir Phillip Coot[84] of Ireland a younger
family of an honorable stock. In that kingdom his estate is said to
be [f. 2] £500 per annum but that is only in Irish reputation which
in England seldome passes for current coyne. But it seems neither
he nor shee were so unciuile to question one tittle on either side
concerning fortune or estate so far from prouiding for futurity by
settlements, which is a proceedure I should thinke a
demonstration that neither is uery rich for such use to capitulate
and are not afraid to expose their conditions. The marriage
precipitated to a consumation at 8 in the euening and after a
refusall by Dr Tenison,[85] a doctor that was so kind to dispatch the
affair is like to suffer for his irregularity. Wee have received a
letter from brother M[ountague] of your safe arriuall and haue
wrote to Sir George by this conveyance. Wee are still of opinion
that your absence is the only expedience at present against the
maleuolent attempts and prate of this towne and you haue the
approbation of seuerall reall freinds that wee meet with, espetialy
Mr Long who sayes that you haue preserued your self by it, and for
tongues when once sett agoing as they are at present concerning
you no one else could suppress them; and it is obserued in
scoulding that giuing no new occasion is the greatest crosse bite[86]
that can bee. But is a scur[v]y quality that most people haue for
they rather speake ill then good and much rather and sooner
beleaue the former then the latter and not only so are greedy to
that degree as to hunt for it as the most pleasing passtime, neuer

---

[83] *caracters*: OED sb. II. 13. reputations (*Ex.* 1712-1868).

[84] *Lady Betty Brabazon ... Sir Phillip Coot*: Lady Elizabeth Brabazon was the wife of William Brabazon (1635-85), Earl of Meath. *The Complete Peerage* claims that she married 'before October 1686 the Honourable Sir William Moore'. It seems unlikely, from the description given in the present document, that Roger and Dudley North have got the details of her marriage wrong. Lady Elizabeth Brabazon was a distant relation by marriage to the Norths.

[85] *Dr Tenison*: See above, note 39.

[86] *crosse bite*: OED sb. used here in the verbal sense of 'to bite the biter, outwit'; hence 'means of outwitting'. OED gives 'cheat, trick' as the meaning for the noun (*Ex.* 1591-a.1734). This last reference is to Roger North's own *Examen*, the latest manuscript of which dates from *c.* 1714. By then the meaning had become much closer to simply 'cheat' or 'trick'.

suffering such to decay but augment and increas it. This is the
virtue of most of those who pass for good, as for the others the
father of lyes[87] appear in them continualy so that itt is impossible
that innocence should be a protection where there is such an
inclination and villanes to be continualy attempting and
administring subject matter. And be assured that [in] so much as a
candid fame and caracter conduce to a happy match[88] you will
haue a full account of in being now retired for some time, and in
the mean time you will be att ease and sleep which is fair quarter
as the world goes. It is more then probable you will be inquired
after espetialy if there be any of value[89] so considerable to bee
regarded. The rest you know what a pest they are, it is enough in
your case if it is[90] knowne sufficiently there is such a person. After
that the lesse seen the better, and the contrary tends to great
disaduantage and in the meane time as we said, your condition is
easy and in truth envious, wherein your great care should be to
change for the better and not hazard the rest of your life to
discontent and patient repentance which in all probability will be
your lott if it be your fortune to fall into the hands of anyone who
hath not an approued caracter.[91] For of mankind (itt is not in the
other sex) it is nott one in 40 that be siuell much lesse obliging or
haue either so much good breeding or nature to make an other
account of woman then a meer property or conueniency; and you
that haue so much goodness and sincerity, which wee know full
well are lesse able to make a party and manage a wedded interest[92]
then others can, and on the other side there are villaines,
barbarous and unaturall wretches so thick prict[93] amongst the rest
that it is odds against missing them. All this is said with sinceryty

---

[87] *father of lyes*: i.e., the devil.

[88] *candid fame and caracter conduce to a happy match*: 'pure reputation and unblemished moral qualities go well together'. *Candid* here has the sense of pure, innocent (*OED a.* 2. *b.*); *caracter* has the sense of moral qualities, strongly developed (*OED sb.* II. 12.).

[89] *of value*: value *OED sb.* II. 5. *obs.* of worth or worthiness in respect of rank or personal qualities (*Ex. c.* 1330-*a.* 1639).

[90] *if it is*: Roger North has 'that it be'.

[91] *caracter*: *OED sb.* 13. the estimate formed of a person's qualities; reputation (*Ex.* 1712-1868).

[92] *make a party and manage a wedded interest*: the North brothers' meaning is obscure here but they seem to be saying 'make a match (in matrimony) and marriage together serve your own profit or advantage'. *Party* is used here in the sense (*OED sb.* IV. 16. *obs.*): a person to marry considered in respect of desirablity; a match.

[93] *prict=pricked*: *OED ppl. a.* 3. dotted (*Ex. c.* 1520-1748). The meaning is that the 'villaines' are thickly interspersed 'amongst the rest'.

32 LIFE INTO STORY

and integrity to comunicate our experience and obseruation to you that perhapps may not haue so much but may be apt to beleiue better of the world then wee doe or then it deserues.

[f. 2v] But wee are sensible that you may also thinke [it] a continuance of the politick designe of keeping you unmarried. Wee haue often heard that objection and almost as often heard you dispise it wherein we haue had great content. Howeuer it is not to be denyed it hath made us more cautious of giuing you occasion then it may be you were aware of or as it seemes now, was conuenient. But those bonds are some what broken and for the future you will find us more free being resolued rather to incurr your jelosie in that particular then be wanting in our seruise to you. Wee haue had the honor of being trusted and considerably for some that wee haue had no obligation to but that of duty and justice and in that haue not been so unhappy to be esteemed so partiall to our selues to use euen those aduantages of interest that the generality would doo and approue, nor doe wee practize such projects upon our selues, that is one another, and it would be strange if we should begin with you for whom wee haue always had more then ordinary kindness freindship and vallue. Wee haue been apprehensive of some accidents that may haue giuen you occasion to suspect in small instances and of the probabil[it]y that you were not without some suspitions. But wee always thought it better to lett all passe with silence, then to expostulate or use words which conduce only to deuision. I doe not know that wee haue been so unhappy in the grand affair to be guilty of fals measures to you being iudged by the successe of seuerall particulars, nay it may rather be said that some points we haue driuen beyond what was in strict decency justifiable. Howeuer you may if you please consider the circumstances of us according to the rule of strangers. Wee are very well satisfied if you are soe and shall alwayes as far as is possible endeauour to doe you the best seruice wee can and wish you all happynesse; and wee haue assurance of your good hart and spiritt which is the cheif thing at present to be relyed on and wee doubt not but with patience in a small time, the world will goe as you will haue it, in which none shall rejoyce more then etc.[94]

D.N. R°.N.[95] Oct. 1686.

Wee must hear from you often, and you will have diversion this week from Mr Soresbye,[96] which wee trouble you not with.

---

[94] *etc.*: Roger North has 'your most affectionate humble servants'. He also adds the postscript.

[95] The date which follows is in Roger North's hand as is the following postscript.

Document 15
'From Lady Wiseman 2 Nov. 1686'
[in Elizabeth Wiseman's hand]

[Addressed: 'These to the Honourable Mr North at his Chamber in the Middle Temple London']
[f. 2]   Nov. the 2d '86
Deare Brothers

Vpon the reception of your letter, I was mightily surpriz'd at the villiany of mankind, and am altogether of your oppinion that nothing like that could be compos'd any where, but vnder the place aforesaid.[97] I presume amongst good people the matching me to that excellent man,[98] will not be at all enjurious nor to my bussiness; and for others, I value them not. I thank you for the care you have of me, and am very well satisfied with your conduct in my affairs, for I am sure you will doe nothing but vpon good consideration and I hope some of you will continue your fauour by letting me know how square's[99] goe. And in the mean time your letter shall be my study, wherein there are many notable observations, and great truths and I will endeauour to guide my

---

[96] *Mr Soresbye*: He is mentioned frequently in these documents. He was Lady Wiseman's legal adviser.

[97] See note 70 above.

[98] *that excellent man*: This may be a veiled reference to William Paston (1652-1732), 2nd Earl of Yarmouth whom Elizabeth married in St Anne's Church (now St Anne and St Agnes) Gresham Street, on 10 March 1687: ironically, it was a Thursday, the day of the week which Elizabeth had allegedly agreed was an appropriate day on which to marry Spencer. Paston was, in fact, a very distant relation, see note 110. If Paston is the person referred to here, there must be some letter or document missing, possibly the letter from Mr Soresby which Elizabeth refers to below, removed from the sequence because it was not suitable to form part of the case the North brothers were making against Spencer. Cf. the postscript to Roger and Dudley's letter above which refers to a prospective visit from Mr Soresby, Elizabeth Wiseman's lawyer, who may well have come to discuss a proposal from the earl. Mr Soresby did, finally, help to draw up the settlement for this marriage. See also Document 16.

William Paston (1652-1732) became 2nd Earl of Yarmouth on the death of his father in March 1683. His marriage to Elizabeth Wiseman was his second. His first wife had been Charlotte Jemima Henrietta Maria, widow of James Howard, and illegitimate daughter of Charles II by Elizabeth, wife of Francis Boyle, Viscount Shannon. In 1684, as Commissioner for the Customs, Dudley North had refused to support a renewal of Yarmouth's timber farm, a lucrative source which would have assisted the earl's financial affairs. Was the suggestion of a marriage to his wealthy sister a form of compensation on Dudley's part?

[99] *square's*: i.e., the business and news of King's Square, Soho, where her house was.

selfe, accordingly for the future. I had a letter from Mr Soresbie, and also one from Neale which has received the same answer from me as formerly. I prayse God I haue had my health very well ever since I came hether, and as you say the blessing of sleeping quiettly which 'twas impossible for me to doe at London. Sir George and my sister etc., are exstreamly kind, and I hope I shall not be wanting in a return. I am enform'd I should be short to men of bussines, and the weather is now so very sharp that I can scarse hold my pen, and am so ill furnish't with writing tools that I ought to apologize for this; but I know you will excuse all comming from
    Your Most affectionate sister and humble servant
    Eliz: Wyseman
[f. 1v, sideways in the right-hand margin:]
I desire the presentment of all reall loue and seruice to Lady D. North.[100]

Document 16
'Letter to Lady Wiseman 6 Nov. 1686'
[in Dudley North's hand]

[Addressed: 'For the Lady Wiseman att Sir George Winneues house at Brettnam. Leave this at Mr Battlys Apothecary liuing in the Cooke row in St Edmunds Bury to be forwarded']
[f. 1]   London the 6 Nov. 1686
Dear Sister
    I doubt not but you haue been displeased not to have from us by last (I cannot say post, but conueighanced by Mr Plumstead), all the blame of which I must take on my selfe, who very reuerendly when it had been signed and sealed ouer night [I] forgott its deliuery next morning. Therein was a letter from my sister Foley[101] which goes now inclosed in this, the former that conteined it being growne obsolete.
    Wee haue great satisfaction in the letter received from you by the hands of Mr Soresby in answere to our long letter and dear sister be assured that wee will neuer neither aduize nor doe any thing in your concernes but with mature consideration and joynt consent. And shall as well consider the speedy as the well fre[e]ing you from the present incumbrance. But tho wee haue been euer since

---

[100] *Lady D. North*: i.e., Dudley North's wife, Ann.
[101] *sister Foley*: i.e., Anne Foley, née North, their sister who was married to Sir Robert Foley.

your departure in a kind of calme yet wee cannot but expect some further attaques before the storme be quite ouer. Your prudent retirement was a thing which they little dreampt of which has giuen them a shock and made them at a stand what measures to take. But my Lord N[orth] is returned, their councells are full and they will come to some resolution which doubt not but will soon be seene in action[.] My Vnkle John Lawly[102] gaue Nan Barret[103] and Betsy Chute[104] a visit and told them that [f. 1v] my sister North told him that Mr S. would insist on the contract and that she and her lord would witnesse it, and when my cozens justified you and seemed to reflect on my Lord North for that bussinesse, he was displeased and discoursed so that they understood themselves reproued for being too forward in beleiuing and made too much of scandall on that noble lord. Vpon this Nan Barret leaues him with Betsy Chute and takes his coach and giues a visit to my sister North, who not withstanding to her said not one word of the pudding. Tother day a person left a message for my brother Mount[ague] to meet a gent at a certaine tauerne butt neither name nor occasion so he tooke no notice thereof and the same day a gentlewoman was to inquire after him and you, but tho he was within would not stay to speake with him. Whether those matters haue relation to your bussinesse [I] cannot tell, but know not any thing else can be meant by them. People will scarce beleiue but you are married and to Sir John T. tho wee affirme the contrary. Indeed the manner of his going off and taking away of his writings, must beg leaue to say, was not according to the laws of knights and ladyes as they are set forth in the most authentick romances.

Brother Mount[ague] has been with Vnkle John and has prepared him to [f. 2] encounter Lord North, and [I] hope ere long shall hear how it workes.[105] This night Mr Neal was with R.N. but upon diff'rent pretences. He spake of his inclinations of which you are not ignorant and ask't if I would be his freind. I sayd I beloved verily that if he made his addresses, he would loos his labour, and I thought that possibly you might have told him as much; he say'd that you had, and that he was of the same opinion with me. However he would proceed. He sayd he was courted now where

---

[102] *Vncle John Lawly*: I am not certain who this might be. Perhaps he was an uncle of Sir Francis Lawley (see note 1) and referred to by Sir Francis's North cousins in this way.

[103] *Nan Barret*: i.e., Anne Barret, married to the grandson (from her first marriage) of their father's sister, Lady Dacres.

[104] *Betsy Chute*: i.e., Elizabeth Chute, the granddaughter of their father's sister, Lady Dacres; see below, note 211.

[105] The letter is continued in Roger North's hand.

he courted before; they stay'd four hours for him to conclude, but would not attend. Intending etc., he will make great proposals, you shall pay detts, and you shall have double of what you purchas, to make ducks and drakes with. He sayd he had so good intelligence, to know you were not engaged to Sir J.T. nor any els. He spoke of the ill usage you have had, and named from whome.[106] Wee al drink your good health and all the good company and rest.

Your loving brothers and humble seruants

D. North M. North R⁰. North

Pray[107] tell Sir G. that R.N. will write to him about some buissnesses that he thincks are forgot.

My[108] wife particularly presents her seruice to you, your little godson beggs your blessing.

D.N.

Document 17
'Sis. W's letter. Nov. 10 1686 received' dated 8 November
[in Elizabeth Wiseman's hand]

[Addressed: 'These to the Honourable Sir Dudley North, at London']
[f. 2] Deare Brothers

This day being the 8th instant I receiued your letter and as you say was much concern'd I had it not yesterday, by the way of Plumsted, for two reasons. First because it came later, and next, every letter I haue by the post stands me in two shillings, so that I desire (if it suite as well your convenience) that I may haue it so without exstraordinary business hapen. I perceiue the L[or]d and L[a]d[y] N. continue still my friends, and will doe me what kindness lies in their power; but I hope God almighty will deliuer me out of such hands, and that it shall not be in the power of oathes to enjure me. I was writt a pleasant story the other day, which for your diversion I will here ensert. Mr S. and the Lord N. went to make a ladie a vissit, and it seems the L[ord] took notice of a two handed fauour[109] in Mr S.'s hatt and askt what wedding he

---

[106] The next sentence is in Dudley North's hand again.
[107] This sentence is in Roger North's hand.
[108] This sentence is in Dudley North's hand.
[109] *two handed fauour*: the meaning of 'two handed' is not clear. The 'favour' Mr Spencer wore was a ribbon, or cockade, which was worn at weddings as a sign of goodwill (*OED sb.* 7. *b.*). Perhaps Elizabeth Wiseman means that he had two 'favours' (one for the bride and one for the groom) which gave rise to bantering

had been at. He said A private one, and withall turn'd to the La[dy] N. in some passion, and said when he came home he would cutt it off. What a stirr there was about it. This became him so exstreamly well, that it gaue the La[dy] N. occasion to discourse concerning his beauty, and ask't the other ladie's oppinion, and withall told her that he was to haue been married to a ladie of a great fortune but when he saw her, he could not like, and so the match broke off. The woman you writt me (made enquirey) I fancy was from Neale for there was such a one at my house, which sent a message from a gentleman of great estate without a name, and I heare by severall he has made it much his bussines to hunt after me, and told Mr Soresbie (by great endustrey) has at last found where I am which I sent him [f. 1v] word should be to no purpose. I had brother M.'s letter last Wensday which do thank him for they being great comforts to me in this condition, and I pray euery weeke for good news that I may look home, tho Sir George and sister are very obligeing, and I haue been very well eversince I came, till this day, I am strangely afflicted with the head ach, which I impute to the coldness of the church, and there being no stirring out without being wett shod. I wonder Lady N. should say nothing of her affaire to cosen A. Barrett. I beleiue she was affraid she should haue as good as she brought, and durst not encounter ... [leaf torn]. I suppose if it be possible my vnkle shall beare a part in this noble designe. [I] pray giue my seruice to all and excuse this tedious impertinent scrible as coming from
   Your most really affectionate sister and humble seruant
   Elizabeth Wyseman

Document 18
'Discours concerning Lady W. 8 Nov. 1686'
[in Roger North's hand]

[f. 1] I[n] Westminster hall about one, I mett Mr Peregrin Bertie,[110] and after some discours of indifferent matters, he say'd he

---

about brides and grooms and made him react so angrily.

[110] *Peregrin Bertie*: brother of Robert Bertie, Earl of Lindsay and Lord Willoughby of Eresby. Their father was Montagu Bertie whose first wife (mother of Robert and Peregrine) was Martha, widow of John Ramsay. Their paternal grandmother was Elizabeth, daughter of Sir Edward Montagu, first baron Montagu of Boughton and Roger North's mother's aunt by marriage, his great aunt. Roger North refers to Peregrine as 'coz' (cousin) in Document 20 although the word does not strictly apply to the relationship between them: the word was used more loosely for relationships in the seventeenth century. William Paston (1610-

understood that my Lord N. was like to be a very great man under the interest of the Lord S[underland] who was very much his freind, upon account of the buissness with Lady W. and that it seems (as he sayd) that the Lord S. prosecuted that matter, and that the Lady W. was gone to Staffordshire, as he understood from the Lord N. or some other place which his lordship knew not, to the intent he might not come where she was, becaus he could convince her that she lov'd Mr Spencer, and bring her to comply with the match. And he sayd seriously that if wee opposed this match, it might goe very ill with us, especially brother D. but the said lord told him, that if the match had gon on, brother D. might have bin made a viscount, and I anything, and all would have run high in our family, which may be brought about yet if wee will. I ask't, as seriously, if brother D. might have bin a vicount, which put him past his retention, and in much laughing he assured mee that the said lord was very confident of it. And I thinck he sayd, Tell your brother of it, and that if he does sell his sister, he be sure to sell her for somewhat. But the nois in the streets did a litle obfuscate this period,[111] but I took the sence so. Our discours was much larger, and he related what extravagant favours the lady shewed the gallant, which the Lord N. told him, that (he say'd) he was afraid to tell mee, they were so much, even to hinder marr[y]ing any els. Vidilicet, that they were alone together 5 hours, and his lordship saw Mr S. lovingly snatch kisses from her, which she repulsed with, fye naughty Mr Spencer. And that they were agreed to marry, the licence provided, and a day appointed, and that the lady desired the gentleman to buy a wedding ring. This last being news I ask't it againe, and he vowed the lord told him so. After all this I thought it my duty to tell him what past. The first visit determined her against him, and she forbad his entrance for the future. Prevailed upon to sup. Rud[e]nesses. The extorted promis to goe to Tooting, fruitless endeavour to hinder it. Witness taken. Last voyage to declare. The sending for Mr S. etc., and after perpetuall attempts that forc't her out of towne. He say'd she had done very well. He asking where she was I sayd At her sister Weneev's with whome she had bin bredd; and I proposed whether it was kind to marry a sister, to one of an unknowne fortune, without an article of provision for her. Hee at that smiled and shaked his head. I say'd wee had great regard for the Lord S. and

---

63), grandfather of the 2nd Earl of Yarmouth (i.e., the earl who eventually married Elizabeth Wiseman) married a Lady Katherine Bertie, daughter of the Earl of Lindsay.

[111] *period*: *OED sb.* II. *b. obs.* the concluding sentence (*Ex. c.* 1530-1769).

knew him to be a man of such honour that he could not thinck wee did ill, to countencance our sister in such an affair as this was, which wee should doe as farr as was honnourable, be the consequence as it would. Ay say'd he, you doe well, and you ought to take care of your sister. This is the substance of what past which I write for memory sake.

Document 19
'10 Oct [i.e. Nov.] 1686 discourse with Lord North about sister Wiseman'
[in Dudley North's hand]

[f. 1] London Wednesday the 10 November 1686.
My Lord North about 6 in the euening came to my house to give mee a visit, when after some ordinary discourse of the news of the towne then he asked mee when I saw my sister Wiseacre. Wiseman I suppose you mean said I. I have not seene her since the morning she went out of towne. Why said he is she out of towne? Yes, replyed I; said he, I thought she had not been out of towne. Then after a considerable pawse he asked mee whether she was gon. I told him immediately to Suffolke to Sir George Winniue's, when he pawsed againe a good while and clapt his hand on his knee and said she had don the foolishest thing that euer woman did, and againe presently after that The thing she had don would make my mother's[112] ashes blussh if they could understand it. I said I know not what he meant and if she had don any thing ill I was sorry for it but I hoped she had not. After which wee sat still a good while and spake not one word, one to other when falling into other discourse in little time he tooke leaue and went away.

Document 20
Letter from Roger North to Elizabeth Wiseman 10 November 1686
[in Roger North's hand]

[f. 1]   10 Nov. 1686
Dearest Bess,
    I intend to trouble you onely with relation of what title-tatle has come in my way, relating to your self. Since our last, I happned to

---

[112] *my mother*: i.e., Anne North, daughter of Sir Charles Montagu of Boughton and Mary Whitmore who died in 1680.

turne a litle in Westminster Hall with our coz Peregrin Bertie, and after the comon questions and answers about news etc., he say'd he heard that the Lord — was to be a very great man by the favour of the Lord S. — and it seems it was upon account of his promoting a match, between you and Mr S. which, he say'd with a serious face, the Lord S. prosecuted. And therefore, as a freind, advised us, especially Sir D. not to be against it, for the Lord N., whome all along he cited for his author, say'd it would be resented much to our prejudice. But on the other side wee might be what wee would had the match taken effect; Sir D.N. should have bin a viscount, and I, any thing I suppose under a viscount, and might be yet, and our family should florish at the top of preferment, if wee should conforme. This being an overture of greater consideration then I had met with yet, I ask't as seriously, should then Sir D. have bin a viscount? which broke the composition of his countenance, and in full laugh say'd For certein and that I might tell him so, for the Lord N. knew it and told him so. But say'd he When you doe sell your sister, I suppose you will be sure to have somewhat, or you will not doe it for nothing, or to that effect. He run over all that stuff that the Lord N. talks to none but folks, of your being in love with Mr S. and fond in an high degree, which he say'd, was such that he was afraid to tell it me, but I prank't[113] him to it by acquainting him with the very truth, which made him stare. He say'd that the Lord — say'd otherwise. And that you were together 2 hours, and he saw the spark snatch kisses from you, and you cry'd Fye fye Mr S. you are naught. And that afterwards you joyned hands, and a wedding day was appointed, and in the mean time you desired Mr S. to provide a ring. But the licence was ready before. So that, say'd he, I don't know whether she can marry any els. He inquired whether you were gone, which I told him. And that you found the impertinence of some and treachery of others such that you could not endure it, and therefore had retired to your sister's with whome you had bin bredd. I ask't if he thought it reasonable, for a brother to match his sister to a yonger brother not worth any thing without a line wrote to provide for her. He say'd that wee did well to take care of, and to stand by our sister, with somewhat more to that effect to no porpose to trouble you with. He had before ask't if you were married to Sir J. T[horold]. I sayd not. Then he spoke a litle concerning his estate that it was about £1500 per annum which they knew being his neighbours, and he say'd it that wee might not want information. This agrees with the

---

[113] *prank't*: *OED v. obs. b. fig.* put in order (*Ex. c.* 1440-1676): here the meaning is 'I provoked him into it'.

account I had from my agent in Lincolnshire, that in a former marriage particular it was given in, at £1700, whereof 100 was improvement. He say'd the dett was about 6 or £7000. After parting with him, my next gossip was Sir T. de Vaux,[114] who yesterday [f. 1v] dined with me, and was wonderfull full of news from Whitehall where he say'd the discours was cheifly concerning you. A great many wagers were lay'd that you were marryed to Sir John Th[orold]. Some yeilded, other[s] compounded, and some were so hardy to stand it out still. It is thought that you retire for some time for reasons best knowne to your self, and then intend to come out, and owne your marriage. It is found out that you took coach at your back door and that it was my coach. And for a blind a hackney stood with 4 horses at your foredoor; this is square news, as I guess by the complexion.[115] The other stuff about Mr S. Ile not repeat, but whereas it is pretended[116] that the Lord N. was to have great preferrment, (he say'd) to be a viscount, the Lord S. had bin ask't about it, and denyed he had made any promise att all, onely being informed his letters would doe a kindsman a kindness, he wrote them in ordinary forme.[117] But Mr S. gave out promises, and declared he would fight any man that should offer to address her. He spoke of Danvers, and his good qualitys, and pretensions to which he is a well willer as I perceiv by his calling him cozen. How he was repulsed by the servants, to his great amazement. And of Neal. None of 'em knew where you were, some say'd at Wroxton,[118] and great inquiry was made who lived there, and kept

---

[114] *Sir T. de Vaux*: he is later referred to as Sir Theodore de Vaux. Sir Theodore (1628-94) was a physician, having been awarded a D. Med. degree from the University of Padua in 1655 (incorporated with the University of Oxford in 1668). He was a Fellow of the Royal Society, was knighted in 1663, and made an Honorary Fellow of the College of Physicians in 1664. He was physician to Charles II and Queen Katharine. Besides knowing him from court circles, the North brothers might have known him as a neighbour since he lived in Covent Garden. Roger North was living there too at this time, renting the house that had belonged to Sir Peter Lely whose executor he was.

[115] *complexion*: OED sb. I. 7. *fig.* quality, character (*Ex.* 1589-1843).

[116] *pretended*: OED v. I. 7. put forward as an assertion or statement; alleged (*Ex.* 1610-1839).

[117] *in ordinary forme*: 'in form' (*OED form*: sb. II. *b*.) means 'as a matter of merely formal procedure'. The meaning of the phrase here seems to be that Lord Sunderland wrote the letters as he wrote other official letters and that they had no special significance.

[118] *at Wroxton*: people might have thought Elizabeth Wiseman would go to Wroxton which was the home of her late brother, Sir Francis North (1637-85), the Lord Keeper. Dudley and Roger North went often to Wroxton at this time to see to their late brother's affairs.

the hous; and understanding none but a steward, it was wondred you would venture, for some were preparing to come downe. I beleev that place considering the neighbourhood[119] will be the last. They beleev'd that after the terme I would goe downe and keep you company. Some say'd you were gone farther, to Sturbridg,[120] 100 miles off, and that it was too great a journy to follow. And, as I plainely perceived by him, most, and the best, concluded by your retirement, that you would be too cunning for 'em all, and have none of 'em, which to me was great satisfaction, becaus it shews that the discours begins to turne in your favour, which was too much before bent the other way, and would have continually increas't so long as you had bin in their way, to administer opportunity to them of giving perpetuall new occasions of talk. And I doubdt not but this will proceed, every day more advancing to your satisfaction. I am apt to thinck that the lord may be so fond to make you a visit, becaus he hath declared that you are concealed for fear he should see you, it being a plaine case, that if he could discours you but 1/4 of an hour, he should convince you that you loved Mr S. and dispose you to be just and marry him. This is one of the items I had from our cozen B[ertie]. I trouble you with naming authors, that you may be assured I write no romances. Wee tell every one where you are, that asks it being not a thing fitting, that one in your rank should be concealed, as they call it, nor doth it sound well to your self, nor freinds, to have your residence concealed. Brother D. will acquaint you that he had an opportunity of making the circumstances of your affaires knowne to the D[uke] and D[uches]s of Beaufort,[121] who are freinds, and of great account. Sir Th.[122] hath promis't me to give me an account of what he hears, and he says he will speak with the Lord N. himself. Such people onely that are tatlers, can give an account of tatling, and so farr will be usefull. In the mean time the value of it is to be considered accordingly. The yong gentleman wants his [£]100 still, and if you pleas to lend it him, you will oblidg him wonderfully; it will help foreward his amour. Mat. J. to whome the proposition is brought, pleaseth himself with bantering upon the subject when

---

[119] *considering the neighbourhood*: Wroxton is near Hanwell, the home of Robert Spencer.
[120] *Sturbridg*: i.e., Stourbridge in Worcestershire, the home of Elizabeth's sister Anne Foley.
[121] *the Duke and Duchess of Beaufort*: the Duke of Beaufort was Henry Somerset (1629-1700). He was a distant relation of the Norths and had been greatly admired by their elder brother, Francis the Lord Keeper. See North, Roger (1995), pp. 66-7.
[122] *Sir Th.*: This is presumably Sir Theodore de Vaux, see note 114.

the scrivener comes; and that he has often appointed, that he might take his diversion. You will excuse all this nonsense from
    Etc.

Document 21
Letter to Mr Oliver from John Fortescue 11 November 1686
[in the hand of John Fortescue]

[Addressed: 'These to Mr Oliver the elder in Sturbridge']
[f. 1]   Ipsley the 11 of November 1686
Mr Oliver
  Pray doe me the favour as to send me word by the bearer, whether the Lady Wiseman be att Mr Folies, and how long shee will stay there. Pray doe me this kindnesse and you will much obliege your freind and servant
    John Fortescue
    A Roman Catholick
Ipsley about halfe way betwixt Wroxton and Stourebridge.

Document 22
Letter to Elizabeth Wiseman from Dudley North, Mountague North and Roger North 12 November 1686
[in Mountague and Dudley North's hands, Roger North has signed his name at the end]

[f. 1] To the Lady Wizeman   London adj. 12th November 1686
Dear Sister
  I am sett downe to write you butt can't tell what or where to begin. Hitherto here has bin litle stirring which was the best we could hope and our proposition succeeding so well, first in stilling those idle tongues and people, whose sole businesse was in plotting aboutt and designeing on you, and then in giueing needy Spencer time to cool and feel his wants, and those who assisted him time to repent and consider their folly and we hoped they would finde how litle able they were to bring about what they designed. We want not our spies and finde the towne fops begin to cry - Igad she has giuen us the horse to hold, the widdow is too wize for us, and wheras before they were ready to cast lotts, now begin to finde you'l haue none of their needy extravagant debautch't worships. The wize part of the towne highly applaud your conduct in retireing as the onely remeady left to gett clear of these rude and indigent people, from whom all things were to be

feared, that man can abuse a woman in. Lord North is now here and I sett Uncle John[123] on him from whom I haue not yett had any account how things haue gone butt beleiue in a day or 2 I shall hear. Brother Roger has a long story to write of what our cozen Berty told him. If things had gone on brother Dudly might haue bin made a vicount and b[rother] Roger any thing. Butt Berty's councell att last was best, that if [we] did sell our sister, itt might be for something. The Lord be thanked, the world is something altered, from huffing, Look too't, look too't, and such like: to be made vicount is something better. Butt the divell of itt is, that 'tis all from the same hand, so all lyes much a like, and lesse hopes of the one then were fears of the other. You are yett here the great discourse of court and towne so you must yett giue them time to digest their former foolish thoughts of you, and on the other side to clear the other businesse. Nothing butt temporizeing, can show us what is fitt to be done, and till that be clear, you cannot with honor nor safety hear new offers. I saw Sir J. Tho. att a play, who has bin asked after you and says he knows nothing of you, nor whither you be or be not in towne. [f. 1v] He is the same man I ever saw him and if any thing, more gay and truly methinks he does not seem to pine much for loue, or lay to heart the misfortunes he unknightlike left his lady in and to labor under. We all liue here as well as we can and want onely your good company to perfect our enjoyment, which if itt were consisting with your good and cirucmstances be assured we would not want one hower[.] Butt we must haue patience, these being things that will not be driven butt must haue due time given them to work and mature of themselves. My humble service to Sir George and his lady and all the family, and the like from Sir D. and his lady. To hear from you sometimes how you enjoy your health were most acceptable. Be assured I am
    Dear Sister
    Your most affectionate brother and humble servant
    Mountagu North
[in Dudley North's hand]
My brother North was last night at my house to give me a visit. Wee stood at bay and scarce spoke 3 words in half an hower, at last he asked when I had seen my sister Wiseacre, meaning you. I sayd not since the morning you went out of towne. He would scarce beleiue but you were in London still. At last he asked mee where

---

[123] *Uncle John*: presumably the Uncle John Lawly mentioned earlier. But the Norths had an Uncle John, their father's brother, who might be the one referred to here.

you were; I told him immediately. Soone after he fell into exclamations of your great folly etc. So wee parted I not thinking fitt to say more to him who pretended[124] himselfe so ignorant, but expected a handle from him which his lordship thought not fitt to glue mee. Wee haue received yours wrote the 8th and are very glad you are well, tho perceave Suffolk dirt is not very pleasant. Wee all hartily wish you outt of it, but something must first [f. 2] proceed and seing my Lord North and his lady are so retentive as not to talke to us tho so lauish to others. Wee haue thought that to make the brazen head speake,[125] you should write it a letter and wee will deliuer it and see how he looks. To this end wee haue agreed of a draft of a letter which goes inclosed which pray peruse and if you like thereof write it ouer and send it open to us and wee will see how it workes. By this he will be forced either to deny or owne. If he denyes, you are safe; if he ownes, then propper remedy must bee thought of. Dear sister wee thinke of you perpetually and this conueighance you will not want diuersion from all of us

D North M North R⁰ North [each signs for himself]

Document 23
'Robert Foley somewhat touching Lady W. Nov. [13] 1686'
[in Robert Foley's hand]

[Addressed: 'To the Honorable Roger North esqr. att his chambers in the Middle Temple London. These']
[f. 1]   Stowerbridge 13⁰ November 1686
Dearest Sir,
I am very sorry to see our s[ister] W. is still persued, for yesterday being this townes markett day a countrey plowgogger that lives near Sir John Hughburnes brings the inclosed to a neighbour of mine who is a butcher by name Thomas Billber,[126] who not knoweing its meaning sent the bearer to me, who desird to know how long my Lady W. did stay here and when she came. My

---

[124] *pretended*: OED v. I. 3. a. obs. refl. professed, claimed (*Ex. c.* 1380-1680).
[125] *Make the brazen head speake*: the brazen head was a legendary brass head that could speak and was omniscient. The most famous in England was that made by Roger Bacon. It was said that if Bacon heard it speak he would succeed in his projects; if not, he would fail. While he slept, the head spoke three times: 'Time is'; then half an hour later, 'Time was'; then another half hour later, 'Time's past'. It then fell down and broke to pieces (Brewer). Dudley North here refers to Charles North as the brazen head, the 'oracle'.
[126] MS has 'Blliber'.

answer was my lady was not come yett, but I expected her about 3 or 4 dayes hence and when she came I could not tell how long she might stay here. It was the best answer to the present question I could thinke of; if I was mistaken, it was want of judgment. Pray let me heare from you, and give me some directions in case the sparke sends another foole on his arrends. I inclose this to Mr Winchrest to you least it be intercepted, to whom I have sent another bond of 8th due from Tho. Dixe of Oxon. which I desire the trouble of you to deliver to Mr Hawkens to gett for me as he gott the other, and it will be an addition to all the favours I have had at your hands which shall ever be acknowledged by Sir

Your most affectionate brother and faithfull servant
Robert Foley

Let mine and my wives humble services satisfie your brothers D. M. etc.

Document 24
'Lady Wiseman's letter to DN 8 [i.e. 15] Nov. 1686'
[in Elizabeth Wiseman's hand]

[Addressed: 'These For the Honourable Sir Dudley North at London']
[f. 2]   Brettenham: November the 15th '86
Deare Brothers

I return you millions of thanks for the fauor of your letters which are now the great'st comfort of my life. I doe exstreamly approue of all the ways and methods you haue taken in my vnhappy bussiness and acknowlidg it a blessing, to have so good and faithfull advice which I will ever adherr to, as the wisest course I can take. I hope it will not be long before things will be in so good a condition as that I may look home because the weather has been pretty seveare, and pinches more then at London by reason we are not provided with winter clothes. My coatchman has been ill eversince I came and not well yet; the rest complaine. Brother Munt. and Roger's letters are mighty deverting, especially to see the case is so well altred;[127] from Look too't to offers of viscount, lords etc. Sir Theo. d'Vaux will be an excellent man to

---

[127] *the case is so well altred*: see Tilley, C111 who cites the first reference ('the case is altered') as George Whetstone's *Promos and Cassandra* (1578). The phrase is also the title of a play by Ben Jonson, first printed in 1609 but probably first acted in 1598. Thomas Fuller also gives it as a proverbial saying in Shropshire, see *Worthies* II. 254. where he ascribes it to the lawyer Edmund Plowden.

discourse with being a man conversant all ouer the towne. There is complaints made by Mr Neale of brother Roger that he takes mony and will plead no where but in Chancery for him. I have transcrib'd the letter to Lord N,[128] and long to know how it will work. I think it the most probable way could have been found out to bring matters to a push, and indeed tis not fitt he should be suffer'd to talk so largely, to other people (without our taking notice of it): and nothing to those that are able to answer him. I hope he will write to me in return of mine, and not attempt to see me here; for I resolue if he comes not to admitt him. I haue not ought else to trouble you with but Sir George's and my sister's service to all and accept the same your selues from, deare brothers
Your most affectionate sister and humble servant
Elizabeth Wiseman

Document 25
'Copy of Sis. Wiseman's letter to Lord N. Nov. 15 1686.'
[in Mountague North's hand]

[f. 1]   Brettenham November the 15 1686
My Lord
Haueing a little recollected my self in my recesse here, where I haue enjoyed sleep and quiett, which I was a strainger to sometime before I left London I cannot butt complain to you, a brother and the head of our family, of the hard usage I haue mett with, nor can any one blame me as hauing brought itt upon my self, when they shall hear that the pretended[129] faults I am to be charged with were committed under your roofe, where I thought my self in a double capacity under your protection. Whither can a poor woman goe or where be safe if not in a brother's house and in a brother's company, where reservedness is not so strickly required as in other places. Yow cannot be ignorant of the threats I had of being seized in the street or where ever he should meett me, in the church or any where else, *upon pretentions*[130] *of a contract forsooth* and since I haue bin here I hear he continues the same discourse still. Butt this is not what I am to complaine to you of, these are rudenesses poor women are liable to. What is more strainge, unnaturall and scarce to be beleived is, as I am told, that you and your lady are wittnesses. Brother, I thought I might haue

---

[128] See Document 25.
[129] *pretended*: *OED ppl. a.* 3. fictitious (*Ex.* 1727-1884).
[130] *pretentions*: *OED sb.* 1. claims (*Ex.* 1425-1855).

expected protection from you and not ruine and I cannot butt beleiue so still. Therefore I write this to require itt from you and that you would not suffer or att least not be assisting to any that shall endeavor to doe this evill to me. I know my self so well and my owne actions that I defye malice and dare stand the test of the severest law. Butt such things haue not come on the stage in our family and I should with sorrow be brought to itt. I shall be glad to hear from you that report has bin a liar in what I haue heard concerneing you and that instead of endeavoring to force me to marry the man I hate, you will contribute to free me from all attempts thereto by others. I haue begged my brothers to waite upon you to deliver this, who I hope will favor me therein and transmitt your answere to me who am your Lordships humble servant.

Elizabeth Wyseman

A true coppie of my Lady Wisemans letter to the Lord North.

[About this time, Charles, Lord North, wrote to their relation (a distant cousin) who had come up to London, Sir Henry North of Mildenhall, Suffolk, recounting his version of the affair. It is clear that he knew Sir Henry had heard another version of the affair, and his own letter was to justify his, and Lady Katharine's, role in the case. Roger North was very earnest in wishing to have a copy of the letter. He feared that Charles North had misrepresented his sister's case. He speculates about the letter's contents and asks Elizabeth to try to get a copy of it when Sir Henry visits her at Sir George Wenyeve's house: see Document 41. Elizabeth reports in that Document that Sir Henry North refused to show her the letter because he claimed that he had no authority from the writer to do so. Nevertheless, a copy of the letter survives among the North papers:[131] it was perhaps supplied when Sir Henry realized that the affair was to be contested in court. It is, therefore, put in the sequence of documents at this point, its place in the chronology, despite the fact that this gives the modern reader an advantage over the original actors in the affair.]

---

[131] The copy appears to have been made by Sir Henry himself (or a scribe working for him) since the signature at the end is in the same hand as the rest of the letter and is not that of Charles North.

Document 26
'Copy of Lord N.'s letter to Sir Hen. North 16 Nov. 1686.'

[f. 1] Sir,

I am nothing alarum'd at my sister Wiseman's winter journey to Brettenham, for the wind blowes where it lists, but fearing some preiuditial stories may be scatter'd causelesly among my neerest relations, and nearer freinds, I think it my part in short to relate some passages lately past between a very worthy gentleman, and her ladiship, and shall omit many of good purpose knowing her pardon will be safely granted, since it is to her advantage. About 6 months agoe my sister and I discoursing about pretentions[132] of marriage dayly propos'd to her she very much inquired about one Mr Spencer, then vtterly vnknowne to me. One of the name I had heard on (a souldier in command) but vppon my saying, I thought she neuer would follow a camp was told, it was none such, but a yonger brother of the Hanwell family, which I knew not but was desired to inquire after the man. About 2 monthes since, the said man came to me importuning my good word, and introducing to the widow. I prepared his way, telling her of his fortune. She willing to see him within a day or two. The interview was much to the satisfaction of the parties, she desiring the matter should not so fall off. Within some dayes she came to my house (where she desired matters might be transacted) where the amours proceeded and thence by appointment with a day to Tooting, where after a short dinner and long wo[o]ing, many expressions of mutuall delight, and geniall salutes were openly in the balcony. Home wee return'd, and after an houre or two parted, his handkercheif without grapes carefully welcome. She on Friday sent by all meanes to see my wife who indeede hauing other affaires, would haue put it off, but she returning that however she would venture, and the gallant being at hand, she was with him till some houres within night. I heare 'tis reported she was lock'd vp, contrary to her will, but who let her out? I am sure neither wife nor I, who tho much dissatisfied by the liberties she tooke with one not then her husband, yet thought it none of our business to disturb louers. At length the doore opening and a Fy vppon ye Mr Spencer, implying intimacies which I cared not to inquire further of, I joyn'd hand in hand, and telling them I was for the country

---

[132] *pretentions*: the meaning here is closer to the noun 'pretender': *OED* 1. b. obs. one who aspires to the hand of a woman in marriage, a suitor (*Ex.* 1612-1728). Here 'pretentions' may be offers of marriage, or aspirations of, or designs upon her by, would-be suitors.

on Munday following, added God blesse you both, and since 'tis thus pray marry [as] soon as you can. I then also learnt that a day was propos'd be[t]weene them for the consummation but not positiuely agreed to, tho faint denialls, and the forwardness that tho brother Roger out of towne, her brother Dudly knew well enough vppon perusall of deeds, whither titles were good or noe etc. But on Sathurday noe newes further but that she was off the hookes[133] and would not behold Mr Spencer who like a lost forlorne wretch lamented it. On the Sunday morning I sent to know whither she would please to admit a visit from me and when. It was appointed after sermon before dinner, when she express'd greate anger against her loue. He was naught, had vs'd her basely and vnhansomly, would haue etc., but I tooke off[134] that preiudice as loue tricks, passion and the best way was to conclude the matter by a happy marriage, which was not denied, and I was told, Mr Spencer needs not be soe hasty, there was noe danger[135] of his succeeding, he had noe riuall to feare etc. In the afternoone my wife and Mr Spencer gaue her a viset, and he most kindly entertain'd. My wife left him after an houre or two. But he tarried til very late that night. My wife before leauing them, heard her say ay to the question, whither Thursday should be the day of marriage. But vppon Munday was alarum'd by a letter with a positiue refusall of any more thoughts of marriage with Mr Spencer. All this is matter of fact, much I haue omitted, but wrote this to informe soe true and worthy a freind, least stories should be that wee had trapan'd[136] her into an vnworthy beggarly match, lock'd her vp, and would haue forc'd her contrary to her will. But pray Sir doe you judge. [£]600 a yeare is his present fortune, has a grant certaine as may be of [£]1500 a yeare more from this king, he is heire declared to the Lady Shaftsbury[137] of £30,000 by euery one's estimate, as also to his godfather my Lord Tyuiott.[138] On May next

---

[133] *off the hookes*: OED sb. II. *Phrases*. 15. *obs. e.* out of humour or spirits, 'put out' (*Ex.* 1842-1894).
[134] *tooke off*: OED v. XI. 83. removed or did away with (*Ex.* 1605-1885). Here the meaning is 'dismissed'.
[135] *danger* OED 2. *obs.* difficulty (*Ex. c.* 1290-1526).
[136] *trapan'd*: OED v. *obs. trans.* entrapped, beguiled (*Ex.* 1656-1894).
[137] *Lady Shaftsbury*: i.e., Dorothy, wife of the 2nd Earl of Shaftesbury, Antony Ashley Cooper. She was the third daughter of John (Manners), 8th Earl of Rutland by Frances, daughter of Edward, (Montagu) 1st Baron Montagu of Boughton. She was thus also a (distant) relation of Elizabeth Wiseman's mother.
[138] *Lord Tyuiott*: i.e., Lord Teviot, Robert Spencer, younger brother of Henry Spencer, 1st Earl of Sunderland, so uncle of the 2nd Earl whom Robert Spencer ('the pretender') claims as his cousin.

shall haue a lease for 30 years of 1000 a yeare more. These are great matters. Ask her if his not making all this good was the cause of her leauing him. Tel her not only this, but allso what he further promised, which was to leaue her owne to herselfe, to put off all pretences[139] to it. That purely loue might appeare the motive of his desires. Should haue been made good if she had desired, as allso an infeoffment of any person in the [£]600 per annum to any brother or other person to her vse til all made good. Deare Sir, I adde noe more. Vse your accustom'd goodnesse. Judge not amisse vppon any suggestions whateuer till I can cleare all. I am sure wee are not to blame any wayes, but in performance of her petition, that wee should haue their meeting at our house in Lecester-feilds whence this kisseth your hands from

Your euer most affectionate humble seruant
16th Nou: 1686   North and Grey

Document 27
'For the Honourable Lady Wiseman at Sir Georg Weneev's hous in Brettenham 18 Nov. 1686'
[in Roger North's hand]

[f. 1] Dearest Sister,

Wee sent you last week a full pacquet, the returne of which, being conducted by the 2 hectors,[140] will teiz the point to a declaration with his lordship. When the play is acted you shall haue an account of the success. Wee have inspired our vnkle, who hath teised as much as can be expected from him, and he hath told us that the lord desires he may not be discourst of, nor blamed, and you shall have no more trouble from S. but you may returne to your hous againe. I suspect councell of that kind from thence. I doe not hear that S. says any such thing, but on the contrary continues his claime. And so I have it from Sir T. who desires his name may not be used. He says your gallants have had conversation, and are of opinion you will marry. But they all speak ill of Lord —. Wee doe thinck you are beholding to him for your deliverance from Sir J.T. of which you shall know farther when wee see you, or sooner.

---

[139] *pretences*: OED sb. 1. claims (Ex. 1425-1855).
[140] *the 2 hectors*: From the mid seventeenth century the word hector came to be used to refer to 'a set of disorderly young men who infested the streets of London' (OED). This is the meaning Roger North has in mind here, as a joking reference to his two brothers, Dudley and Mountague, who (we are told at the beginning of Document 28) took Elizabeth Wiseman's letter to their brother Charles.

52 LIFE INTO STORY

They have at last found out that the mares nest is at Brettenham. Capt King prest Mr Wright to tell where you were which he would not, having other measures, from Sir Georg. But lately he came to him in a kind of tryumph, and say'd that now he knew where you were. You know whose neighbour he is. Mr Wright in a very freindly manner told me this, not knowing of what import it might be. A catholick that lives between Wroxton and Sturbridg, sent to a butcher in Holytowne to know if you were there, and the honest butcher brought the letter to the justice, as they call him, and he has sent it to us; and that his answer was that you would be there in 2 or 3 days, to see if any fools would dance. I beleev if you are intended any visits they will be performed in a short time, but I rather thinck that the caracter of your company will prevent them. Your letter is received and shall be faithfully delivered. In the mean time make much of your self, and so lett your servants; colds are as frequent here as any where els. Our services to all, and most especially to your self:
  from
  Your most affectionate humble servants.
  D. North M. North R⁰. North [each signs for himself]
18 Nov. 1686

Document 28
'Narrative upon delivery of the letter to the Lord North 19 Nov. 1686'
[in Dudley North's hand]

[f. 1]   19 Nouember 1686
Friday at 3 in the afternoone brother Mount and I went to the Lord North's to deliuer the letter wrote by my sister Wiseman and sent us to be giuen him and pray his answer. There being company there wee stayed some time in expectation that they would be gon but finding them continue to stay I cal[l]ed my brother aside into the little withdrawing roome, brother Mountagu following, and tooke out the letter and told him that I waited upon him at the request of my sister Wiseman to deliuer him a letter which she had sent open to us and desired to receiue his answer thereunto. He immediately sate downe to read the letter and at euery paragraff nay almost line made some wonderment or other: at some laughed att others denyed to know any such thing and particularly when he came to the word contract he said he knew of

none and that none was pretended.[141] Also when he came where he and his lady were said to be witnesses he laughed, Of what etc. As to the threats of seazing her in the streets there he wondered at it and said he beleued not that any such pretences[142] were. I told him that both the one and the other had been pretended[143] and that Mrs Lane in myne and brother [M's] presence came from Mr Spencer who she said had been at hir lodging to find her out, and told her that Mr S. said he would seize her in the streets, church or any where, whereatt he wondring much and saying he knew nothing thereof I told him that was strange for his footman brought Mr Spencer to Mrs Lane's lodging whereto he said little and only denied [f. 1v] that he knew any thing thereof. This I told him was cause and just one for her leauing the towne, and the pretence[144] of a contract was also true how false soeuer the fact[145] was at which he acknowledged that he had heard that Mr Spencer hearing that my sister had sent to Sir John Thorold to come to her and she would marry him that he sent a gird to Sir John to acquaint him that she was his wife before God and that she was not fit for any man else to haue. On which wee both wondring what should be meant told him that it did not become him to say such things of his sister but that he should take her part when any body else should say soe of her and that what was don or could be pretended[146] was in his house. Whereat he seemed to startle and said that she was aloane with him in her owne house many howers to which wee replyed that his lady brought him thither and left him there against her will and that she had two seruants sitting all the while in the next roome and would not suffer the doore to be shut, the which he partly denied and partly confessed. Hee seemed much to justifye the reasonableness of Mr Spencer's pretentions from his circumstances of estate etc., to which I said I could not beleiue he had the setlement as was said being but a yonger brother, and that now his name had been used to take up £100 joyned with a sword cuttler for security and the pretentions of a great match which were not [f. 2] signes of any great matters, also that another brother I had heard going to sea had uery slender prouissions from home. Wee often told him she was his sister as well as ours and it would become him to take her part and not to

---

[141] *pretended*: OED v. I. 5. *obs.* put forth, claimed (*Ex.* 1495-1755).
[142] *pretences*: OED sb. 5. assertions, allegations (*Ex.* 1608-1856).
[143] *pretended*: OED v. I. 7. b. *obs.* asserted (*Ex.* 1639-1781).
[144] *pretence*: OED sb. 1. the putting forth of a claim (*Ex.* 1425-1855).
[145] *fact*: OED 1. something done or performed (*Ex.* 1545-1815).
[146] *pretended*: OED v. I. 7. alleged (*Ex.* 1610-1839).

endeauour to force her to marry the man she hated at which he laughed and said that wee should not force her not to marry the man she loued. I said I should neuer opose her marrying any man she liked and if she liked Mr Spencer I should not be against it but while I liued I would endeauour to see that she was not wronged or forced to any thing, and that neither large promises nor threats should take mee from that duty in any time or place. He said wee would not suffer her to marry anyone and that it was said at Banbury,[147] that she should not marry as long as wee could preuent it. I said I cared [not] what was said of me nor by whom; my actions should testifie for me. Wee desired his answer. He said he would not fayle to write her and that he had lately given Sir H. North a large account of all.

Document 29
'Letter to Lady W. 20 Nov. 86.'
[in Dudley North's hand, directed by Roger North, signed by Dudley, Roger and Mountague North]

[Addressed: 'For the Honourable Lady Wiseman at Sir Georg Weneev's hous in Brettenham. To be left with Mr Bately at his hous in Bury St Edmonds Suffolk. To be sent express']
[f. 1]   London the 20 Nov[embe]r, 1686.
Dear Sister,

Wee should not haue put you upon the extraordinary charge of a letter this way but that [we] beleiue you are uery desirous to hear a returne of our embassy. Wee, that is Mount and I, waited upon his Lordship yesterday in the afternoone when after near 2 houres attendance for an oportunity he giuing vs none wee were forced to make one and desire his lordship to stepp aside that wee might speake a word with him. When going into the litle withdrawingroom heretofore Mr Closbrookes closet I [set] your letter as by your command and desired his answere. He immediately sate himselfe downe to read it and at euery line gaue att least a start, sometimes a jump, looking wisely and laughing as matter occurred. He told us he could answer it and you should haue it. He seemed mightyly astonished at hearing of violence had been threatned you as seazing in your coach etc., and said [he] beleiued it was false and that no such thing euer was threatned or intended to which I replyed that I was sure it was threatned for Mrs Lane in myne and bro[ther's] company had told you as much

---

[147] Banbury is near Hanwell, the home of the Spencers.

from Mr S., at which he wondered and said he knew nothing of it, which I told him was strange for Mrs Lane declared that his footman brought Mr S. to her lodging, at which he only professed his owne innocences and cleared the matter no further, and this I told him was the cause of your leauing London. As to the word [f. 1v] Contract he laughed at it and said neuer any was pretended[148] and pished at the sa[y]ing he and his lady were to be witnesses. I told him I was uery glad to hear him say soe, but contract or some thing like it I understood was pretended in a message sent by Mr S. to Sir John Thorold at which he laughed and said that he heard indeed, that you had sent to Sir John Therold to come to you and you would marry him, whereupon Mr S. sent a gent to him to let him know that you were his wife before God, and not fit for any one else to have. This amazed us both very much and wee told him wee wondred to heare him talke soe of his sister; it would become him to hinder and preuent others and couer and hide your faults if any and not proclaime them. Wee further told him that what had passed was in his owne house. At which he said that you had him till one aclock aloane in your owne house. Wee denyed that it was so late and told him that his lady brought him thither and left him there against your will and that when she was gon you had two seruants sitting at the door which was open. Wee said he ought to protect his sister from violence of others and not endeauour to force her to marry the man she hated, Hated said he? Pray doe not you (to us) force her not to marry the man she loueth. Wee told him all our ends and endeauours were [f. 2] that you might be left to your owne freedome and if you liked Mr Spencer wee should neuer be against it, but as long as wee liued in all times and places would stand by you that no force should be offered to you. He seemed to justifie Mr Spencer for a uery fit person from all his circumstances, I told him I could scarce beleiue the settlement being butt a yonger brother and heard another brother going for the Indies had very slender prouisions made for him; also I had heard that some body in the name of this gent. was hunting up and downe the towne for £100, offring a sword cutter for security and using for argument that he was to have a great fortune. I beleue he begins to be a little ashamed of what is past for he told us that perceauing the world was poysoned by reports of him he had lately wrote a large narrative for his owne justification of all that had pas[s]ed to Sir Henry North.[149] Now sister nothing can be so well worth your while as to get the originall or a copy thereof out

---

[148] *pretended*: OED v. I. 5. obs. claimed (*Ex.* 1495-1755).
[149] See Document 26.

of which matters may be collected for your seruice. I suppose this night he will write you. If so pray let us haue coppy of it for our gouernment in this affair which will now begin to ripen. If you find that he endeauours to come smoothly off with you as I beleiue he will you must put it upon him to procure from Mr Spencer something under his hand, whereby he may null all pretentions of that nature, and tell him that unlesse he does this for you, you cannot thinke your selfe safe nor used by him as [f. 2v] a brother ought to use a sister. If you find occasion to write him in this manner as I hope you will doe not send it open to us but directly by the post to him, but send us coppie for our gouerment. Wee[150] have considered now being together that there is great necessity that wee should see your letter in answer to the lord becaus there will be nicety in the penning of it, and if fitting care be not taken, advantages will be taken against you from it. Therefore wee shall expect the draught of your answer and returne it for you to direct, in case he writes as he says he will, to give you occasion. Nothing more but all possible services from
   Yours etc.
   D. North M. North R⁰. North [each signs for himself]

Document 30
'Lord North's letter 20 Nov. 1686'
[in Charles North's hand]

[Address: 'These to the Honourable the Lady Wiseman']
[f. 1] Madam
   Much am I amazed at a letter from your ladyship after the grand civilities received when neither accesse to me or mine (tho a brother, an elder brother to whom by God and nature the love and care of the family is in trust) no not a letter could obtain the favour of coming within the angry widdow's door as being a friend to the Spencers forsooth. I am that, dear sister, and your true friend in it whatever suggestions those of your brethren you most confide in can bring righteously against him. And marvell not while you reject him, causlesly, without a why or wherfore after so gratious an admittance that my inke even blushes to imagine. That his resolves are to speake with you and expostulate. Lett him take his fortune after that. Else he threatens an utter removall of those pitifull obstacles stand in his way. For God sake sister he cannot eat you by a word in private and, mistake him not, no rape is intended

---
[150] The following is in Roger North's hand.

nor further suit of matrimony. I have heard him declare you shall not be troubled more as to that (you will not be so happy). He has since applied elswhere and of that I can be a witnesse if it will doe you service. In my house all the matters I can tell of is that after Nay fy upon you Mr Spencer, Nay then quoth I (joining hands) God blesse you together, I am for the country, marry soon as you can, and that you receivd not this civility of mine with reluctancy. Nor had you cause. Your mutuall salutes in the balcony at Tooting were obvious to more eyes as also your familiarityes by the way. How farr these amount to a contract Heaven knows not I. But am sure (for all a proud word) he indeavours nothing in that kind. Once more I importune your giving access to one visit more from him. I fancy not that you hate him. Being a reasonable creature that might expresse for what if there were any cause. More then I feare which is that some seek advantages by keeping you unmarried and the message to Sir John - was without their knowledg and in vaine. Pray consider your wayes and lett it not be sayd of my mother's daughter that ever such imprudencies came from her. Did I doe beyond what you [f. 1v] commanded? Blame me then but tell me wherin. But if both my wife and I never did, nor shall doe but what really is for your good and service lett no false stories separate you from, or exasperate, your best friends. Did we lock you up? Did we indeavour for a man you hate? Are we conscious of any threatnings that drive you from your house and home? No. Know this in spight of your ill usage and froward imaginations that I both am and will ever be your indulgent good friend and loving brother, carefull of your interest, concealing what has been amisse and acting the best I can for your service and no way against you. And therfore, dear sister, take my advise and resolve of a sedate admittance of the gentleman to some words with you in private without the awfull audience of those that have openly declared their intentions to keep you always unmarried. If he has or no the estate given out would have been a handsomer foundation for a breaking off. Would it were now to be prooved. But in the interim believe them vilains that dare tell lyes and asperse a gentleman and not justify it.

Nov. 20th 1686

    I am dear sister
    Yours in all, as I ought
    North and Grey
I direct not this to Bretenham but as you desire,[151] scarce fancying you so farr out of towne.

---

[151] See Document 33 where it is obvious that he has directed the letter to Roger

Document 31
'Robert Foley, somewhat touching Lady W. Nov. [22] 1686'
[in Robert Foley's hand]

[Addressed: 'To the Honourable Roger North esquire att his chambers in the Midle Temple London']
[f. 1]   Stowerbridge November 22 1686
Dearest Sir

Against of the 18th present I sent and thinke my selfe obligd to let you know all motions of the sparke I last wrott of. On Saterday last my men were at worke in my barn fanning of corne, one Bolns[152] a butcher of this towne came and calld one of them out and privately askt if one Lady Wiseman was here, who answered him Noe. Bolns desird if she did come he would give him notice of it. Assoon as I heard of it (which was not till last night) I sent for Bolns who sayes a servant of Sir John Hughburns came from Mr Fortescue and desird him to inquire iff the lady afors[ai]d was here, and Bolns sayes he sent the person upp to inquire himselfe, but I can heare nothing of him. I presume he was the same party that was here on Friday senight, and from the said Mr Fortescue. Bolns tells me he was invited tomorrow to Bromsgrove market[153] to buye some fatt cattle off Fortescue but returnd this answer He wanted none. I told Bolns my Lady [Wiseman] had not been well and this very wett weather had obstructed her jorney but hopt when the weather was better settled she would be here. Wee have had so much raine and the waters have overflowne euery where and my lady durst not venture her jorney as yett. My wife desires the favour of you to send the boy with the inclosed to sister Wiseman. Wee desire to be presented very faithfull servants to her; and am

Sir, your most affectionate brother and obliged servant
Robert Foley

North's address.
[152] *Bolns*: is this the same man to whom Robert Foley earlier refers as Billber? See above, Document 23.
[153] *Bromsgrove market*: Bromsgrove is halfway between Worcester and Birmingham.

Document 32
'Lady Wiseman to us 22 Nov. 1686'
[in Elizabeth Wiseman's hand]

[Addressed: 'To Roger North esqr. at his Chambers, in the Middle Temple. London']

[f. 2] November the 22nd / 86

Deare brothers:

I receiued a letter (according to coustom) from brother Roger which do thank him for, and in answere to it, doe wonder what Captain King has to doe to make enquirey after me or my affairs, without it be occasioned by his neighbourhood. The sending to Holey Town was by Danvers, who, tho he had notice of my being to come thether, resolu'd not to dance so farr to no purpose, but came hether, to as little this morning, where I was willing at last to see him; in the presence of Sir George, sister and neices. The weather being so exstreamly bad Sir G. was willing to giue him the civillity of an ordinary stranger which he could not turn out, at that time of day without entertainment. He declar'd he would be sattisfied if he once saw me, which he shall never doe again wheresoever I am. He would haue whispred some news to me which I would not admitt of. Brother Dudley's account of the carriage of Lord N. had this morning brought from Bury,[154] and doe return thanks for the care and paines hee's been at. I do presume I shall haue a letter from him; and allso be made aquainted of the narrative by Sir H.N. [Henry North] who we haue exspected euery Friday here, now h'as matter for discours and I fancy will come the next. I beleiue he forc'd it, by a letter from him to Lord N. for the countrey is full of storeys, I perceiv, by Mr Harvey that came hether but was mighty reseru'd, only full of laughter. If the lord write to me I shall send it post to you and desire your advise in return of an answere, for where they lie at catch,[155] it tis not safe for me to trust my selfe, and I do suppose I may haue a return by the post soon enough. Neale writes to me all manner of wayes, and fancyes he shall do great matters. I was affraid after the terme[156] he will make a vissit allso, which I know not how to avoyd: but will giue him as cold wellcome as I can. I hope you will pardon this scribled paper, for the truth is the

---

[154] *Bury*: see above, Document 29, which describes Dudley North's letter as being 'left with Mr Bately at his hous in Bury St Edmonds Suffolk'.

[155] *lie at catch*: OED catch sb. 1. b. obs. lie in wait (*Ex.* 1630-1814)

[156] *after the terme*: i.e., at the end of the legal term.

weather is gott into my brains: (which at best are not good) and accept of all loue and hearty seruice from
    Your most really affectionate sister etc.
    Elizabeth Wiseman
[f. 1v, sideways in the right-hand margin:]
I could wish, for my diversion, to have the storeys of Sir J.T.
My most humble seruice to your good Ladie, and blessing to pretty godson.
I am writt of a place, that is a relation of S. where he confess't that those writeings he sent for vp to Lord N. were false, and that he has nothing but £90 a yeare enuetty [anuity] from his father.

Document 33
'Letter to Lady W 23. Nov. 1686'
[in Dudley and Roger North's hands]

[Addressed: 'For ye Honourable Lady Wiseman at Sir Georg Weneev's hous in Brettenham Suffolk']
[f. 1] Dear sister
    Wee wrote you on Saturday night, when [we] did not thinke the Lord N. would haue trusted vs with his answere to your letter, which you by the inclosed see he did, sending it under a couer to Ro. North's that night, where he found it when it was too late for us to meet againe in consideration thereof. The letter being to speake for its selfe, wee need say little. Wee find our selues deceiued in what wee conjectured when [we] wrote you, this conteining nothing like any thoughts of his making fair weather, as then wee hoped he would, but on the contrary, he is where he was at first, capitulating that you should againe admit Mr S. to speake with you in priuate. Saying his resolues are to speake with you, and expostulate. Hee seems to amuse[157] you, that his pretentions[158] are not any longer matrimony, (you shall not be so happy), he has since applyed elsewhere etc. Certainly he can haue no bussiness with you but that, and if he has laid downe the thoughts of that once, he need not presse so for admittance. But wee take this to be only said to amuze you, that he may haue you in his power and then play that game that he likes best, the consequence of which no body knows and is not to be hazarded. As to his pretentions in the legall way, wee all think no danger in that, considering what Lord N. now sayes, whereupon wee think

---

[157] *amuse*: OED *v.* 4. delude, deceive (*Ex.* 1480-1817).
[158] *pretentions*: OED *sb.* 3. *obs.* purposes, designs (*Ex.* 1545-1872).

he cannot doe you any harme that way, unlesse by skaring away them that may apply to you, as was lately the case of Sir John - and this certainely is one of the games he playes. To obviate this, wee haue discoursed to you that a ouit may be brought of iactitation, wherein he must either justifie or be wholly sett aside. But wee now plainly perceaue, that he strikes deeper. Pray what can be the meaning of the message my L.N. sayes Spencer sent to Sir John - that you were his wife before God, and fit for nobody else to haue? and what meanes my Lord N. saying so gratious an admittance that my inke euen blushes to immagine? with expressions of this nature in his former letters, and discourses. I say sister, wee now perceaue the designe is laid at your honor, and I doubt not should a suit be comenced, they would endeauour to perswade the world strange things. Dear sister you see how he [f. 1v] taxes us not only in his letter, but to our faces, that wee are resolued to hinder your marrying any body, by which meanes he hopes all wee say will goe for nothing. But as wee haue promised faithfull councell and plain dealing, wee will, in the name of God, with sincerity goe on so to doe, lett the successe be what it will, or lett it be beleiued of us as it may. And in your case, as wee find it at present, it is our unanimous opinion, that you must not yet awhile thinke of the towne. The circumstances of your affair admitt noe cure, but that of time. Your future well being consists wholly in the mannaging of this affair, and you will find the account of euery daye's stay, in reputation. Nothing but such a resolution, with perseuerance, can encounter the snares you are under and pray consider and vallue the great reputation you haue hitherto had. If you come to towne he will certainly offer violence, and if he has not his ends in that, he will as certainly strike at your reputation, and as this wicked world goes euill tho false, preuailes, and is sooner beleiued then the truth. Wee say in an Italian prouerb. Give mee time.[159] You haue time; make use of it, keep out of the way till this storme blows ouer, it cannot last long.

Wee[160] must desire you to excuse the gravity of the stile, for wee doe assure you the matter in hand is neither in jest, nor capable of any, not such as wee have bin alwais so free to use, as freinds, with mixture of earnest, the more divertingly to insinuate our sence. Never any thing yet has happned in any of our experiences of such

---

[159] *Italian prouerb*: I have been unable to find an Italian proverb which might translate as 'Give me time'. But there is a proverb: 'Dai tempo al tempo', *lit.* 'give time to time', i.e., let things take their course, which might be what Dudley North had in mind here.

[160] The following is in Roger North's hand.

tenderness[161] as this, both in relation to your well being hereafter, which wee most sincerely promote, but also to your, and our honnours, with which it is very hard to comport patiently, if they come to speak plaine, what they now too planely insinuate they mean. Few countrys would bear so much, without what I will not mention.[162] There is no being here, without the test of violence, or dishonnour, one of which, or both you must pass; and if the former takes place the latter will follow of cours. And moreover there are a parcell of harpys waiting for you in towne, who will superinduce[163] their stratagems upon all this, and their continuall inquirys, conferences, and dispers't foolish and malitious conversation, bating[164] the danger to you, when they take for granted [you are] resolved to marry some or other, from attempts that no one can profecy, will be a burthen insupportable and ruinous. In the mean time, as they all confess, you are too hard, and too cunning, for [f. 2] them by your retreat, wherein you have your eas and live without perplexity and torment that hath possession of this towne, against you. You ought, and have great reason, to be pleased that you are redeem'd from the most facinourous[165] damb'd stratagem that ever was formed against a woman. It was realy beleev'd by them, whome I mean, that is no lord . . . . [sic: =?North] that the privacy should have had the success they intended, which failing, wee beleev they resolve not to be loosers, or disappointed in it, but will certeinly drive it out, and depose[166] as if it were so. Judg your deliverance. That now you are escapt, and are in a way of honour and reputation, not otherwise to be preserved. And every day the ignominy devolves upon the authors, which wee find by their daily kicking and wincing. Wee see this and have given you some account of it. Wee hope you will enjoy your health, and likewise all your family but once more, what wee have hinted often, let not your concerne, and consideration about them, impeach your owne conduct of your self, which you are cheifly to regard. If they cannot conforme to your way of living, be it what it will, chang, and take others that will. There is to be no grumbling in these matters, and learne to

---

[161] *tenderness*: OED 1. delicacy (*Ex.* 13..-1856), but used here in a figurative sense.

[162] *what I will not mention*: i.e., a challenge to a duel.

[163] *superinduce*: OED v. 2. bring in over and above (something already present) (*Ex.* 1605-1877).

[164] *bating*: OED prep. leaving out of account (*Ex.* 1568-1817).

[165] *facinourous*: OED a. obs. extremely wicked, infamous (*Ex.* 1548-1871).

[166] *depose*: OED v. 5. testify, esp. give evidence upon oath in a court of law (*Ex.* ?a. 1500-1873).

direct 'em what they must and shall doe, and expect. They serve you, and must conforme to your measures.¹⁶⁷ And as wee were about saying, now you have reason to be very well pleased, that you have scapt a granado¹⁶⁸ intended for your martirization, and to laugh at the folly of your enimys, and not be concerned at all at what is past, but be cheerfull, and light, for all is well hetherto, notwithstanding what they did, and doe still intend; but have bin prevented, to their shame, and so will be. And wee may add, what was told the Lord — at the delivery of your letter, that ne[i]ther promises, nor threats, fears or hopes, should move us from stand[ing] by you, in your defence and protection to the last extremity, being nothing but his owne hand could make the caus of all this credible to any man.
23 Nov. 1686
  Most affectionate humble servants.
  D. North M. North Rº. North [each signs for himself]

Document 34
'Letter to Lady W. 25 November 1686'
[in Roger North's hand]

[Addressed: 'For the Honourable the Lady Elizabeth Wiseman at Sir George Winneve in Brettenham Suffolk']
[f. 1]   25 Nov. 1686
Dearest sister
  This morning S. rose early, (as wee suppose,) and came to R.N. in W[estminster] hall, when happily¹⁶⁹ he was walking with Chute,¹⁷⁰ who knowing him and his designes, therefore prest to observe what past, which he [RN] is pleased of becaus there is one to prevent lying, which is much stirring in these affaires. He (avoiding Chute) prest R.N. aside and say'd his buisness was with him and that was to tell him that he had traduc't him and his family, and he must and would have satisfaction. The answer was, Have I traduc't you and your family? then take your cours, you know where I am, and my walks, and I shall not stirr an inch out of my way for you. Which was all between them. After, he took occasion to walk with Chute, who had an hour's talk with him.

---

¹⁶⁷ *measures*: OED sb. I. 7. b. standards or rules of judgment (*Ex.* 1641-1830).
¹⁶⁸ *granado*: OED = grenade, here used figuratively (*Ex.* 1657-1886).
¹⁶⁹ *happily*: OED adv. 1. by chance (*Ex.* 1377-1890).
¹⁷⁰ *Chute*: i.e., their cousin Thomas Chute. *Cf.* Thomas Chute's account of this meeting in Document 2.

The sume of which is that he hath a full promis of you to marry him, and a day, viz., Thursday appointed by you, being admonished[171] of the matter, so no surprise. But as to his prosecuting or not, he is betwixt hawk and buzzard;[172] much other tatle, too long to account, but Chute acquitted himself very well. This wee look upon as a foolish cowardly buissness, and lay'd in Leister feilds, for an experiment, because Lord — came this afternoon to D.N. which wee suppose (he not being at home) was to prevent mischeif. But wee understand the catle[173] well enough not to fear their appearance in harme's way. Wee have received yours, and doe extreamly approve that of Sir G.'s conduct, and doe verily beleev that in a few such instances they will find you so wise, not to trouble you so vainely as now they are set upon. And take notice you never appeared with so much advantage in your life, as amongst your relations, where your authority, and protection is irresistable. Wee have not time to inlarg, so must referr many things to another opportunity. In the mean time beleev, what air finds us, would be a storme to you were you here. Wee have bin larg in our last, for which there was soe bad a voucher. You must excuse if anything was too much, becaus all proceeds from sinceer intentions in your service from

Services etc., from etc., to etc.,
Your most affectionate humble servants.
D. North M. North R⁰. North [each signs for himself]

Document 35
'An account of what past between me and Mr Spencer, and between Mr Spencer and Mr Chute as I had the same upon discours with him afterwards the same day viz., Thursday Nov. [25] 1686'
[in Roger North's hand]

[f. 1] In the morning at Westminster Hall before the courts sate I was walking with Mr Thomas[174] Chute, and Mr Spencer bore[175]

---

[171] *admonished*: OED v. 5. notified, aprized (Ex. 1574-1855).

[172] *betwixt hawk and buzzard*: Tilley H223 gives this as an equivalent to the saying 'neither fish nor fowl'. But the meaning here is that the choice between two *similar* alternatives is difficult, and so the phrase is closer to 'between a rock and a hard place'.

[173] *catle*: OED sb. II. 7. b. arch. of men and women, mostly contemptuous: vermin, insects etc. (Ex. 1579-1823).

[174] Roger North has 'Edward'. Edward Chute was Thomas Chute's brother.

upon me as if he would separate me from Mr Chute but I was desirous to have him hear what past, and I perceived he was also curious to know, so that such mutuall inclinations brought us almost together againe. But Mr Spencer againe bore ott,[175] and say'd his buissness lay with me, and not with Mr Chute, but still he followed, and was within hearing.

Spencer say'd that I had aspers't him and his family, and he must have satisfaction, or an account why, or some such thing. I answered that if I had aspersed him and his family, he might take his cours, for I would not stirr an inch out of my way for him or any els, and my walks were knowne, and he might speak with me when he pleased, or to the same effect.

Afterwards walking with Mr Chute, he told me severall things which past between them two, for Spencer came to him, and walk't neer an hour and an half. But he could not undertake for[177] any method in his discours, because, as he say'd Mr Spencer was so disorderly and flattering in what he say'd, that he could not give an orderly account of it, but I beleev before wee parted he related most that past betwixt them, which I can less remember, becaus severall days since are elapst.

As to favours, he said he prest Mr Spencer to say what favours they were, becaus that was a doubdfull word and many would understand more then he intended by it. Therefore he desired to know what it was he meant and after some hesitation, and unwillingness he say'd that she promis't him marriage, and that was favour enough, and owned no more, whereupon Mr Chute advised him not to to use that word, without explaining his meaning by it, becaus others might understand more then he did, or wors.

[f. 1v] Mr Chute say'd a great deal to him of the improbability of what he pretended,[178] he having had opportunity by accompan[y]ing her to Tooting to observe all passages betwixt them, and alwais took notice that she slighted and despised him, and gave him no sort of countenance, much less to be fond of him as he would insinuate. And therefore he could not beleev that there could be any such thing as a promise.

At which Mr Spencer was disturbed and shewed some resentment that what he say'd should be suspected of falshood, and, what was more that the Lord N. and Lady, who both sayd and

---

[175] *bore*: OED III. 36. pressed, forced [his] way; with 'on' (*Ex.* 1593-1872).
[176] *bore off*: OED III. 34. *intr.* resisted (*Ex.* 1542-1852).
[177] *undertake for*: OED 10. *b.* engage [himself] in a promise (*Ex. a.* 1715-1827).
[178] *pretended*: OED *v.* I. 7. asserted, alleged falsely (*Ex.* 1639-1781).

declared the same thing should not be beleeved. Which Mr Chute took up, saying, he did not affirme that what any of them say'd was not true, but that it was very improbable, of which he could judg being present in their company, and observed her behaviour, which was so different from any such thing, that he must be excused if he beleev'd rather that some mistake happened then that it should be really so.

Then he prest Mr Spencer to say in what words the promise was, which he was very unwilling to come to. At last after much questioning, he say'd that she appointed a day, viz., Thursday, for her marr[y]ing. At what time? said Mr Chute. 5 in the evening, answered he, and perceiving the time being uncanonicall[179] made a circumstance[180] of improbability, he took occasion to observe that persons of honour had of late affected[181] the time to marry, wittness Lady El. Brabazon.

But Mr Chute say'd it might be very probable that the Lady W. meant no matrymony by that which he might possibly mistake for the appointment of a day, as being ask't whether Thursday were a good day or not, she might answer Yes, and that Wedensday Fryday and all God almighty's days were good, which signified nothing. And it seems the Lady W. had told him that the passage was so in truth.[182]

Mr Spencer declared that his promise was plaine, and no surprise, and she was told that he being a man of honour, meant accordingly, that was matrymony, and therefore she must have regard to what she say'd. So that as to his claime, of a promise he was plaine and positive, and say'd nothing that tended to a renouncing of it.

But as to his suing upon it, he shuffled, and at first exprest himself uncerteinly, but at last sayd that he intended not to trouble her in that kind. Tho his words [f. 2] imported nothing that he was sensible[183] he could not, but that for the honour he had for her he would not. All which I did ask Mr Chute most particularly upon.

Spencer did proffess mighty honour, and respect to her ladyship and that nothing should make him deviate from the strictest

---

[179] *the time being uncanonicall*: the hours between which marriage could be legally performed in a parish church were the canonical hours. These were the hours of 8.00am and 3.00pm. The marriage of Lady Elizabeth Brabazon is discussed in Document 13.

[180] *circumstance*: OED sb. III. 10. fact (*Ex.* 1586-1850).

[181] *affected*: OED v. 2. b. had a preference for (a thing) (*Ex.* 1593-1875).

[182] See Document 12 where Elizabeth Wiseman refers to this naming of days.

[183] *sensible*: OED a. III. 11. cognizant, aware (of something) (*Ex. c.* 1412-1837).

behaviour of himself accordingly. But to be used as he had bin, after he had made his addresses in the way of honour and was so oblidgingly received, to be disappointed, and bafled as he was, could not be borne by a gentleman

As for R.N. he complained that he could not speak with him, which Chute contradicted, saying, There he is you may speak with him when you pleas. And as for Sir D.N. he had used him basely, with more ejusdem farinæ.[184]

Document 36
'Letter from sister Wiseman 29 Nov. 1686'
[in Elizabeth Wiseman's hand]

[Addressed: 'These to the Honourable Mr North of the Middle Temple London.']
[f. 2]   Brett: November the 29th '86
I was mightyly surpriz'd (deare brothers) at the reception of your letter, dated the 23 instant, which enclos'd Lord N.'s who I see is still bent vpon mischeife, but I did hope he would haue giuen me a more sattisfactory answere to mine. What our vnkle said I perceiv proues a flamm, and there is no trusting to such cattle.[185] I neuer read such stuff but from the same hand, nor is it fitt to be answer'd, but in the languish [sic] of Billingsgate,[186] which is below me to medle with. If you see him, and haue an oppertunitie you may tell him that. As to his proposeition of my admitting that villain S. I will never doe it whilst I breathe nor see his face more if I can avoy'd it and for haueing a minutes discourse with him in private! I will sooner submitt to have my body torn a peices by the lyons then be subject to his ensolence and withall defy him, lett him do his worst. He talks to cosen Chute of promises etc. As I hope for mercy there was neuer any such thing: and as to the message he sent to Sir J.T. viz., that I was his wife before God and fitt for nobody else: I vow to God I know no more of it, then by a repetition of that rudeness I formerly aquainted my S.D.[187] with which I am sure who soever hears, will acknowlege I haue sufficient ground for my implacable hatered of him. I hope you

---

[184] *ejusdem farinæ: Latin* lit. 'of the same flour', here, something like 'of the same nonsense'.
[185] *cattle: OED sb.* I. 1. *e. fig.* rubbish, trash (*Ex.* 1643).
[186] *Billingsgate*: a fish market was held near Billingsgate in the city of London, and was noted for its vituperative language.
[187] *S.D.*: Sir Dudley?

will be so much my friends, as not to be concern'd at what Lord N. (in malice) sayes against you vpon the account of my not marrying: I know, and am sure, I haue had sufficient proofes to the contrary: and this is only an envention to revenge himselfe vpon you for being my cinseare and true friends, and I hope you beleiue mee to haue more sence then to mind it, and have formerly heard me declare against the vileness of any such thoughts. I know and am sattisfied you all wish me well: but for the enventour of these lyes he w[ill rejo]yce I am confident (and as appeares [f. 1v] by his actions) to see me rhewened: but God almighty I hope will deliuer us all out of their and such like hands. For God sake take care of your selves, tho I hope there is no danger in such a fellow's hectouring, and I look vpon it to be a cowardly trick, as the last exstream hatch't in the place aforesaid.[188] I am told no body in London giues creditt to their false reports, and doe hope it will in time dye to their shame. Danvers made us another vissit: and surpriz'd me in the parlour, but before he could gett in saw me make my escape, which convinc't him 'twas purely my own act which before he was so weake as to think was constraint. He came towards the evening and shamefully beg'd a lodgeing of Sir George with a promise of setting out early the next morning. It was a courtesie in these ways was not to be denyed to a gentleman [but] it putt a force vpon me of keepeing my chamber, so that his lodgeing was no way to his sattisfaction, not seeing me all the time he was in the house. He pretended he had much to say in private conduseing to my service, but I would admitt of none of [it and I] doe hope shall heare no more of him. R.N.'s clyett [i.e., client] Mr Neale has tormented me with severall loue letters, all which I haue enclos'd to Mr Soresbie to deliuer him, by which if he be a reasonable man hee'l be sattisfied. I am affraid I haue been too tedious with you as I ought not to be with men of bussines, but 'tis fitt to be read when you haue nothing else to doe. For Godsake when you are together, consider whether there be nothing to be done in honour to silence this rascall. I haue enclosed this letter[189] to putt amongst the rest, and if at any time you think fitt it should be otherwise answer'd, lett me haue what I shall write. Servi[ce] from all to all.
    Eliz. Wyseman.
Mary Howard is a pettitioner, to Master Munt for a little of his snush [snuff], to cure her toothach.

---

[188] i.e., in Leicester Fields, Sir Charles North's house.
[189] i.e., Document 30, Charles North's letter.

Document 37
'Letter for Lady Wiseman 2 Dec. 86'
[in Roger North's hand]

[Addressed: 'For the honourable Lady Wiseman at Sir Georg Weneev's hous at Brettenham in Suffolk']
[f. 2] Dearest sister,

Wee being together at D.N.'s and wanting your letter, were impatient, and sent to Mr Plumsted to know if there had come any from Brettnam to him this week, and the carrier being just come in, and he reading his owne letter, sent us Mr Soresby's pacquet, wherein wee found one to us, and we sealed up the rest and sent to him.[190] I know the impertinence of client Neal, but he cannot say that he has any incouragement from his learned councel,[191] but the contrary in plaine English, viz., that he was clearly of opinion he would doe no good. He say'd he was of the same mind, but for all that would goe on. I heard that he mett his cosen[192] Sp. at Lady Tivertts and told him that he was mistaken in his pretentions, for he intended to carry the lady himself. Sir T.[193] tells me that Sp. hath bin introduc't to another rich widdow,[194] by the Lord, but more especially by the Lady — and that several visits have bin made, but no advances yet, which will be entered into proposition now very suddenly; I should give consent to marr[y]ing, or hanging, no matter which, but the match-brokers declare his estate shall be made out to the outmost. Wee shall take care to keep the precious text such as no age, person, nor invention, but his owne, can paralell. Wee know very well that certeine tongues are no slander; and so it proves; and your absence heaps coles of fire upon 'em; for all cry shame, that you are oblidged, which all agree you are, to retire from treachery, and impertinence. As for their censures, and huffs, relating to us, you know very well how much

---

[190] In her last letter (Document 36) Lady Wiseman said that she had sent Mr Neale's love letters to Mr Soresby. Is Roger North making clear that he scrupulously did not read these letters, presumably enclosed in the packet for Mr Soresby?

[191] *learned councel*: This is Roger North, who seems to have been doing some legal work for Neale in relation to a matter involving Elizabeth Wiseman, possibly the borrowing of money.

[192] *cosen*: This is the first mention of Neale's being a relation of Spencer. Does Roger North mean this, or is it a sarcastic reference to their common desire to gain Elizabeth Wiseman?

[193] *Sir T.*: presumably Sir Theodore de Vaux.

[194] *another rich widdow*: See Document 48.

wee scorne 'em. No less then wee did the hogan-mogan[195] applications wee had, with respect to your concernes, and had they bin threats the same receipt they would have had, much less are either the words and actions of such trifles to signifie any thing. But you may see how low the buissness is reduc't to come to such sorry methods. Sir T. says he will write to you, there will be no harme in that, but he is a spy of Danvers. I have made him promise to tell you all and plainely what he thincks may concerne you that comes in his way, how he will acquitt himself I cannot tell, but he is a profes't scrible, and will divert you. Wee were of the same mind as you are, that the letter[196] is not fitt to be answered but with detestation. Wee hop't to have the narrative sent to Sir H.N. which wee suppose is made of the same meal for indiscretion is such to make no distinction of persons. We have not time to trouble you much at present, having but the intervals of claret onely for scribling, which is more then once diverted with your health. But next week wee shall be more larg and particular. In the mean time wee desire you will not thinck us tired with anything from you, but the greatest disappointment is brevity. Mo[untague] has sent a present of snuff to his old acquaintances. Service to and accept the best from

Your most faithfull humble servants

D. North M. North R⁰· North [each signs for himself]
2 December 1686.

Document 38
Described by Roger North as '2 letters from an unknowne freind'
[4 December 1686][197]

[Addressed: 'Theis to Counceler North att his chamber in the Temple']
[f. 1]   December the 4 - 86
Mr North

I have grate news to tell you which I could not forbare letting you knowe which will sirprise you. Mr Neale is fully resolved to haue the Lady Wisman your sister: in order to it is gone to hir to Catetlidge Hall where I sopose he had incuradgment from hir to come. I doubt not but my Lady may thinke he may make a good husband which I beliue he may, as a gentleman. As it is reported

---

[195] *hogan-mogan*: OED a. B. 2. *obs.* high and mighty (*Ex.* 1648-1705).
[196] *the letter*: i.e., Lord North's letter to Elizabeth Wiseman, Document 30.
[197] See also Document 40.

and seartanily trew that [he] has in his house a young gentlewoman this two or three years which the wourld dos say grater kindness can never haue bine then betwixt them. Sir I haue giuen you this trouble, make use of it as you thinke fit from

Your unknowne frend

Document 39
'M.N.'s account of his visit 5 Dec. 1686'
[in Mountague North's hand]

[f. 1] Being in the playhouse within 2 seats of Lord North assoon as he saw me we passed due salutes. Between the acts he leaned over to me and told me he would be glad to speak with me about that businesse to which I replyed with all my heart, I would waite on his lordship where and when he pleased, when he appointed next night, which I think was Sunday night 5 December. When I went and found his lordship all a lone by the fire, when telling I was come to waite on him according to his order we imediately fell to the discourse of our sister Wiseman, when his Lordship began to speak much in the prayse of estate and person of Spencer and his relation etc., which discourse I cutt short by saying, that our sister had received his lordship's letter and had wrote us and declared she hated Spencer so much that she would be torne in peeces by wild horses, rather [than] haue any thing to doe with him and was resolved never to see him more, soe that we were to serve her in the way she proposed to be served and no other way, which was to clear her from the trouble and inconvenience she was under by the pretensions[198] of Spencer to promises, which were so false. Then Lord North said that Spencer denyed what was said was sent to Thorold and that he never spoak of her butt with the greatest honor and respect imaginable.

To which I replyed that I was glad to hear Spencer carryed himself so justly to our sister, butt she was a silly[199] woman and afraid of trouble, so that if whilst Spencer was in this good humour his l[ordship] could procure from him a declaration under his hand, it would be to the satisfaction of our sister and a favor.

---

[198] *pretensions*: OED 1. allegations or assertions the truth of which is not proved or admitted, often with the implication that it is put forth to deceive (*Ex.* 1609-*a*. 1984).

[199] *silly*: OED 1. *b. obs.* defenceless (*Ex.* 1587-1665).

He imediately said itt should be done and that he was sure Spencer would giue itt on his first asking itt, and therfore ordered me to consult my brother Dudly and R. and send him itt and he would write itt outt in an other hand or cause itt to be writt and we should haue itt. I told his lordship 'twould be requisite to haue 2 wittnesses att which he was concerned butt I saying his lordship and one of his foottmen might see him signe itt, would be enough itt was soe resolved on. [f. 1v] But his lordship and my self seeming to desyre that this thing might be kept private and espetially from his family where if I came 'twold be known there was something extraordinary doeing, his lordship appointed to haue the writing brought to the coffe[e] house neer Whitehall[200] sealed up and left for him in a letter whither he would be sure to send for itt by nine of clock on Twesday morneing, and so itt was agreed.

On Munday ith afternoon L[ord] N. came to R.N.'s chamber in the Midle Temple who being busy his l[ordship] went into the inner room, when accidentally I came in and went imediately to him, who L[ord] N. told me he was come to tell us, that he could not procure from Spencer the writeing he had promised, Spencer saying he would not giue them ease who had giuen him so much trouble. Butt his lordship sayd he did beleiue and was certaine he would never sue or giue her more trouble aboutt itt, to which M.N. made some reply butt his lordship was in such hast to gett away he beleiues he did not hear him.

M. North

Document 40
The second letter
[6 December 1686]

[Addressed: 'Theis to Counceler North att his chamber in the Temple present']
[f. 1]   Munday morninge
Mr North

Satterday eveninge I made bold to giue you the trouble of a letter which this is to intreate the favour of you to lett me speake with you in the eveninge if you please to apoynt your time and place: if you leave the place to me I would desire it may be att the Dog

---

[200] *the coffee house neer Whitehall*: This may be Man's Coffee House, mentioned in Document 56.

Tavern in Drury Lane number two:[201] att your owne time. I intreate the favour of an answer by the carr[i]er. I hope you will not refuse this kindness it will be satisfaction to yourselfe and oblige
    Your vnknowne frend

Document 41
Letter from Elizabeth Wiseman to Roger, Dudley and Mountague North 6 December 1686
[in Elizabeth Wiseman's hand]

[Addressed: 'These to the Honourable Mr North at his chambers in the Middle Temple London']
[f. 2]   December the 6th 86
Deare Brothers
    On Thursday last Sir Henry N[orth] was here but could not be prevaild with to giue me a veiw of my Lord N.'s letter. Of it, he told me, of my Lady N.'s hearing me say Fie (in my own house) to Mr S.['s] proposeition of being married on Thursday, and magnifying his estate, beyond what was ever said yett, viz., that the king had giuen him £1500 a yeare, that he was to haue a lease of a £1000 a yeare more for 30 years very suddainly, from whom I know not; that he was declar'd heyre to the Countess of Shaftsbury, of £30,000 personall estate, and that he had great exspectation from his godfather, Lord Tiveot, all this besides [£]600 a yeare settled on him by his father; with somewhat more, not materiall. And the reason why hee's so nice[202] in exposing my lord's letter, is first (as he sayes) because he hath noe commission so to doe, and next because in preudence he ought to be tender in doeing a thing which possibly may make the breach wider, which he hopes, is not so, but that in a little time it may admitt of a cement, and I am assur'd by Sir H.N.'s friend that there is no new thing in the letter but a repetition of what I haue had formerly, from himselfe, and by you. Only one thing which I look vpon as a new envention, which is that the lord sayes I was the first that spake to him of S. and prayed him to find him out and gett him for me. To this I answere, that by way of discourse I did mention the name, before I

---

[201] *Dog Tavern in Drury Lane number two*: I have been unable to trace this particular tavern, although the name appears to have been common. 'Number two' is the number of the private room presumably booked for the meeting. This system of booking by numbers allowed anonymity as well as privacy.
[202] *nice*: OED a. 5. b. obs. shy, reluctant (with *in*) (*Ex. c.* 1560-1676).

knew what he was; because he had been very troublesome, by some weomen coming to my maid, and I told him I lookt vpon him to be some idle person, by his address that way. At this he began to stare, and said he knew none but a soldier: What, would I follow the camp? and this storey he now makes of that, to palliate his own crime. There is no reflections vpon you more then you haue heard, which will be impertinent here to mention but a world of nods and winks and etc., which he cannot bring out for feare his ink should blush (I supose) and leaves Sir H. to guess at ... deale, more then ever ... it to amuse him. [leaf torn at bottom] [f. 1v] but for all that, he is really sensible of the abuse I have had, from the Lord N. He sayes he designes to eate Xmas pye with him at Catt[lege] this Xmas, and then, he will try, when he has him alone to make him sencible, for he looks vpon this as cheifly, transacted [by] the vertuous lady so fauourable an oppinion has he of his lordship. I wish he may doe [well] in it or that I were married or hanged or somwhat that I may be looking homeward. I thank God I am very well in health and exstreamly civilly vs'd by Sir George and [my sister] but [I am] affraid I shall encomode them when their house will be so very full [at] Xmas. We haue this day had a vissit from Mr Neale who came out of London early Satterday in afternoon, lay at Bury last night and was here by dinner, to my great surprize: for I did hope he would not haue done it, hauing had no encouragment from me, tho he threat'ned. But I hope he is gone away sattisfied with his doom (as he calls it) which he would not accept from any but my own mouth. He carried hemselfe very obliging to all, and took formall leaue of me, so, that hee'l be the occasion of no further trouble I hope. The seruants here, pray for him, for his mony flew amongst them.[203] He came with a coach and 6 and greatly attended, return'd after dinner to Bury where he design'd to lodg, and will be at London, again before hee's mist. You see I doe not loue brevity, by this tedious epistle, but haue much adoe to find stuff to ramm it with. But you ought to be larger, considering you are three, to one: your enventions more copious, and the place you are in will better afford it. I shall haue a world of rattle from Sir Theo.[204] I suppose (if he writes) which will be very diverting. Pray pardon the errors

---

[203] *his mony flew amongst them*: i.e., he was generous in giving gifts to the servants.
[204] *Sir Theo.*: Sir Theodore de Vaux.

of this and accept of my hearty seruice to you all from
> Your most affectionate humble
> seruant Eliz. Wiseman
> seruice to all etc., from etc.

Document 42
Letter from Roger North to Elizabeth Wiseman 9 December 1686
[in Roger North's hand]

[f. 1] 9 Dec. 1686
Dearest sister,

An unknowne freind, in a woman's manner, wrote a letter to R.N. to advertise that Mr Neal had declared he would marry the Lady W. and was gon downe to Catlidg hall on porpos; and she could not beleev he would expose his reputation in such a voyage, unless he had some considerable encouragement but it would be unhappy to a poor woman if such should prove a match, she being betrothed to him before God, and would perish if such a misfortune should happen to her, as to loos Mr Neal. This letter was regarded as a flam but seconded by another from the same hand, pressing to speak with R.N. where he would appoint, and if the place might be left to her, it should be the Dog tauerne in Drury lane, Number 2. This had the cast of an assignation of which good use might have bin made; but the apprehension of a trappan[205] deverted that vertuous designe, and he acquainted the porter, that the chamber was the place where such as he was to be spoke with, and there he would wait upon her when she pleas'd. Not long after her ladyship came with [a] female attendant. She was well drest, and not unhansome, - her subject was the same as in her letter, but more copious, as you know weomen doe more freely discours, then write. She say'd much of the distressed condition the poor lady was in, beleeving Mr Neal with the beautys of his person, and witt might prevaile; the rather becaus the Lady W. being at present in some trouble, might in a sort of despair marry any one. But she said, all was not gold that glitters, and much to the disadvantage of Mr Neal, in respect of his estate and health. And she hoped the Lady W. (whome by the way she often called Lady North) when informed of the interest[206] of another person, would not doe an act soe injurious as to marry Mr

---

[205] *trappan*: OED sb. 2. trap, snare (*Ex.* 1665-1823).
[206] *interest*: OED sb. 1. claim, in this case with the sense of 1. *a*. legal concern *in* a thing (*Ex.* 1450-*a*. 1680).

Neal. That the lady was already so disturbed at the apprehension of it, that she would neither eat nor drink, and they dared not leav [her] alone, for fear she should make away with her self. She sayd Mr N. had notable intelligence, for a knight at the Tower corresponded with some hostesses on the road, and had sent him a discovery that you were gon to Catlidg in Suffolk, neer Stowmarket. And that Mr Neal was certeinly gon after which brings to memory the verses in Hudibras, - of ladys purloyn'd and knights persuing like a whirlewind.[207] The sume of what was say'd to her was, that it was beleev'd that neither had Mr N. any encouragment, nor that he would prevaile which was all the satisfaction could be given to the sick lady. But she would have a promise that you should know of this, which was granted, and is complyed with and it is beleev'd that it was the sick lady her self that came of her owne errant. Little news since the last of Lord O.[208] who useth to be very teeming of monstrous impertinences, till Mt. [Mountague] was an idle fellow, and went to a play, where the wheel of fortune plac't him next his lordship who had full imployment in mangaging ... [the paper is torn at the fold] The onely discours that past betwixt them was a [request] of the lord that he might speak with the gentleman about half an hour [about] that buissness, which was understood, and complyed with and lately Mt. went to his hous. His discours was still advocating for Mr Sp. upon the subject of his person, witt, and what exceeded all his fortune. But Mt. would not enter into debate upon those points, becaus not materiall in the present state of affaires, for you had since the receit of his lordship's letter, wrote one to us so full of detestation of him, that were he an angel, wee could not thinck of any other way of serving you then in your owne way, to ridd you of a fellow that you hated. His lordship say'd much of the great honour and service he had for you and that he alwais exprest himself accordingly, and there was nothing he would not doe to serve you, and that he had given over all his pretensions[209] of marriage. Thereupon Mt. thought of taking the opportunity, and if it might be to get a note [f. 1v] of him to that porpose, and say'd that if he was in so good humour, his lordship would be well to procure of him some declaration in wrighting to that porpose,

---

[207] *verses in 'Hudibras'*: Samuel Butler, *Hudibras* (1663-78) Part II canto 1, ll.13-14:
    Some writers make all ladies purloin'd,
    And knights pursuing like a whirlwind.
[208] It is presumably Charles North who is referred to as Lord Nought.
[209] *pretensions*: OED sb. 4. obs. aspirations (Ex. 1620-1782).

which would be a great service to you, and justification to himself. This was no sooner hinted, but he with wonderfull readyness and confidence undertook to get of him any note that wee should prepare, and appointed time and place, to have it brought, and he would transcribe it, and of this he was pretendedly[210] so sure as to make no doubdt. But the place must not be his owne house but a coffee hous. Lady Dacres,[211] it seems, being come to towne had hufft[212] him at such a rate that wee beleev he would have bin glad to get ridd of the buissness, of which more anon. The next day, his lordship condescended up 2 pair of staires to R.N.'s chamber, where Mt. happily was, who instantly waited upon him. And his buissness was to declare from Mr Sp. that he would [not] give any renunciation of your engagements to him. But his lordship's opinion was that Sp. would never sue, then tost[213] away; and R.N. had not the honour to see him. There was the exit of that buissness, whereby it appears that upon consideration and consultation they are upon the same what-she-call'um project still. And since Lord O. hath hinted that it will be best not for you to sue, for what may follow, which was at a meeting at Lady Dacres, of which more anon. First of Mt.'s visit and mine. When imediately she crowed in victory over the lord, and told how she had subdued him, upon the abominable point in his owne hous, obligation, and relation. Wee acquainted her of some matters which she had the lord's denyalls ready for; and wee appealed to papers of your hand [and] his hand to demonstrate what wee say'd was true. And sayd brother D. intended her ladyship a visit next day, and should shew 'em to her. She was mightily upon the rant[214] at an impudent fellow, that should offer to come in her doors against her will; she would kick him out of the hous. And then turned her and stampt. She approves of your being in the

---

[210] *pretendedly*: OED adv. professedly (*Ex.* 1611-1851).

[211] *Lady Dacres*: Lady Dorothy Dacres (1605-98) was the sister of Elizabeth Wiseman's father, Dudley 3rd Baron North. She was always referred to as 'Lady Dacres' by the Norths although Lord Dacres was her first husband. Her second husband was Chaloner Chute (*d.* 1659). Her daughter by her first marriage, Catherine, married the son of Chaloner Chute by his first marriage (i.e., her step-brother Chaloner, *d.* 1666 age 36) and by him had four children: Chaloner (1656-1685), Edward (1658-1722), Thomas and Elizabeth. Thomas Chute is the 'cousin Thomas Chute' referred to in this case and 'Betsy Chute' (Document 16) is Elizabeth.

[212] *hufft*: OED v. 6. trans. scolded, chided (*Ex.* 1674-1862).

[213] *tost*: OED v. III. 7.b. flung (himself) (*Ex.* 1728-1852).

[214] *upon the rant*: OED does not give this phrase, but for *rant* sb. 1.b. obs. a violent scolding. The phrase means something like 'enraged'.

country, to be out of way of an impudent fellow; but she says you ought to scorne, and despise him and all that he says, lett him say what he will, at your heels. And as for any renuntiation of his, she would despise the thought of it, and never give him so much credit as to take it, if it were offered. You may remember that when his proposition of an enterview came, with that in the taile of it, that he would give a note of discharg, wee were apprehensive that if you closed with it, he would have a better pretence[215] from that, then any other, as if it shewed you were sensible[216] there was need of it; and thereupon you resolved not to admitt him upon any termes. Now wee thought that such a hint coming from Mt. to Lord N. might at least discover their resolutions, if not take effect, and it plainely shews that he never would have done it. Nor if it hitt to be ask't for the reason wee have touched. Wee told her that you resorted to her as a parent[217] of our family, to countenance us and joyne with us in your protection, which she vows to God, she will, to the utmost. She ask't why wee did not say this, and that, and shew this and that to the lord and S. and scorne 'em and their pretences[218] to their faces. Wee say'd wee had not the priveledg of their ladyships to talke it out. Wee should sooner goe from words to blows; but wee never stuck to declare the plaine truth to all that gave themselves the trouble of being informed from any of us and so could allwais doe. She inquired of Sir J.T. and wee told her how farr it went, and being in treaty for £1000 per annum rent charg, which he stuck at [and] had not agreed to. This matter gave him occasion to break off. She ranted, that so litle was ask't and say'd that your owne fortune would buy as much inheritance, which is more then joynture. Wee say'd wee hopt that would [f. 2] shew wee were not against your marr[y]ing provided you had a man you could like, of honourable circumstances. As to him,[219] wee cannot give you particulars. Wee had a generall advice sent from one whose understanding in generall and knowledg of him in particular is not to be questioned, nor her freindship to us, and yourself. The name you may hereafter know, but at present it is under too great an injunction of secrecy to be inserted in a letter. There have bin other advices of the same import, as freindly, and without any malice to him, but not of so great account as the former. The plaine truth is his manner, the occasion taken, and

---

[215] *pretence*: OED sb. 1. claim (*Ex.* 1425-1855).
[216] *sensible*: OED a. III. 11. aware (*Ex.* c. 1412-1837).
[217] *parent*: OED sb. 2. obs. kinswoman (*Ex.* a. 1450-1771).
[218] *pretences*: OED sb. 5. allegations, assertions (*Ex.* 1608-1856).
[219] *As to him*: The person referred to here is probably Sir John Thorold.

the time of leaving, is such as you that know it, cannot but have a right sence of. Wee are told that his sister the fair one, was pleased to say she was glad her brother did not sacrifice himself to one of your years, but she spoke plainer, and this comes from one that heard her say it. You may beleev it, nothing but advantage was sought, and after that secured and made his owne, to have the least trouble with you that was possible had bin his game. Wee parted with Lady D. and this day, the 8th December D.N. visited her with all his tackling of papers in his pocket, and whether by appointment or chance doth not appear, a lord[220] was there. And such a scene it was, as never did I hear any thing like. The buissness was to fend and prove[221] upon matters of fact, befor the Lady D. who sat as judg and you know the lord never wants matters of fact to alledg. The main of which was that all that he did in the affair of Sp. was at your desire and direction, that it was not suddainely transacted, but depended[222] a long time; that you were fond etc., stuff you have bin nauseated with too often. There was D.N. like a lawyer with his bundle of breifs; Say you so quoth he. Here is your owne hand to the contrary, and there is her hand to the contrary, here are dates of letters, and circumstances in wrighting that shews times etc. Every one of which, (and so many and such instances and passages of confusion were there, not possible to be particularized or described) made him stare, gape and gogle, and rune to new facts then new answers. So that all the most minute circumstances that really are in your affair, were fully discussed, and proved on your side beyond possibility of denyall. In the mean time, so hott and fierce were they, as to come very litle short of right downe railing; or wors. He would affirme that the dates of letters were forged. Then, said D.N. I must forg 'em having had the custody. Perhaps you did say'd he. And in short to the teeth of him,[223] he made the true reflections upon the whole action, and set it out in its proper[224] colours. Had wee bin all present, a better account had bin given; but the secretary [i.e. R.N.] having onely a relation, thincks no better manner of describing such a ... [paper torn] conflict, then by wrighting nonscence such as

---

[220] This was Charles North.
[221] *fend and prove*: under *fend, v.* 2 *intr.* the *OED* gives this phrase: argue, wrangle (*Ex.* 1575-1877).
[222] *depended*: *OED v.* 7. was waiting for settlement (*Ex. c.* 1430-1883).
[223] *to the teeth of him*: i.e. Dudley North confronted his brother Lord North. *Teeth* here has the *OED* meaning of directly to his face, with the sense of confrontation or opposition, *OED sb.* III. (*Ex.* 1542-1724).
[224] *proper*: *OED a.* II. 4. *obs.* accurate, correct (*Ex. c.* 1449-1875); that is 'true colours'.

you read, for confusion and scold was the whole enterteinement; and then he left him to the scool of the Lady D. All this shews your deliverance, and happiness in being secure from outrage and violence; wee cannot but understand this proceeding as a full and plaine declaration, that no means whatsoever, civil and uncivill will be unatempted to get you into their power, hoping thereby to justifie themselves, as well as gaine your estate, which is their point; and wee cannot thinck you in any sort safe from destruction, and misery in this towne nor any where els out of the company and cohabitation of your weomen relations, and as your affairs stand, it is not in the power of us all to secure you any eas or thought of safety, without your being surrounded with weomen relations [f. 2v] as well as men. And therefore wee cannot without infringing the sincerity and plainess wee have profest always to use in communicating our thoughts to you, decline to acquaint you that it would be very convenient that you gave notice to part with your hous as soon as you can; wee thinking it absolutely impossible you should live by your self. For setting aside this intregue of Sp. the blades have an opinion you are so bent upon marr[y]ing, that he that presseth with most forwardness is most like to prevaile, and you are look't upon as one of the good things now to be gott, and they are to blame that venture not for it, as much as to loos a preferrment for want of solliciting. And it is impossible suddainely to cure such fancys. Saying the contrary, is talking to the wind; time, and a contrary cours of life must doe it, nothing els. It is unhappy when it so falls out, you know whome to accuse. But being so, the proper[225] cours must be taken. And it is most important for you to consider, what vast disadvantage you would have in case you should, having a fair proposall, marry, being under these circumstances. During your whole life it would be made a reproach to you as if you had outstayed your patience, and were forc't to comply with anything which a litle ill nature would improve to your no litle inconvenience. Therefore you are not to thinck all this time lost, but the best imploy'd that could possibly be contrived to make the rest of your life happy. Wee cannot see what the sequel may prove. Perhaps some very favourable opportunity may emerge, conducing to your perfect satisfaction. All good is to be expected, so long as no harm can happen to you in the cours you are in. And your discours ought to be formed in the stile[226] of the greatest contempt imaginable of

---

[225] *proper*: OED a. III. 10. in conformity with social ethics, respectable. (*Ex.* 1704-1852).

[226] *stile*: OED sb. II. 15. manner of discourse, or tone of speaking (*Ex.* 1567-1875).

these workers of wickedness; and in generall against marr[y]ing, which wee have often say'd upon former occasions. And in confidence of your truly understanding our intentions to be sincere, wee venture to say all this, so lyable to misconstruction. None beleevs a widdow, maid, or batchelour that declares against marr[y]ing. But in truth it hath a double convenience 1. to thro off impertinencys, and 2. to dispose the better to advance, which it most certeinly doth, as the contrary averts. The world is of this composition, and ever was, and will continue so. Such is a style[227] unexceptionable, for every one hath power to dispose themselves, without giving any reason, for it. All other reasons are either exceptionable or inconvenient. It is mightily desired by them that you should returne to London, to no other intent but to ... [page torn] your former practises, with more cunning and efficacy. You know how to take advice from enimys who they say, and truly, are the best councellours. It is not their aim to oblidg or gratifie you. There hath bin no such footsteps yet, but to gett what they call good. Wee desire that you will use the same freedome with us as wee doe with you and if anything occurrs to your mind, which you thinck probably expedient, let us know it, and wee will most honestly give you our thoughts of it, that desire nothing more then your good. And after all, that is it which is at stake. You must consider, and judg of your owne affaires, and determine, for all the consequences are yours, wee doe but present you with our sentiments, for your information, and all possible endeavours for your assistance, whenever wee thinck either may be of service to you.
    [Letter unsigned: a copy]

Document 43
'Letter to Lady Wiseman 9 December 1686'
[in Roger North's hand]

[f. 1] Wee know very well it is insinuated all the towne over, and the sparks will scarce beleev the contrary, that you are under a force,[228] and Lord N. affirmed the same to D.N. before Lady D. [Dacres] and that you still lov'd Sp. and would declare it if you were free. Which you may imagine he flew in the face of, and defyed, shewing how fals, and nonsensicall that was. Then, sayd the lord, but you correspond with her; and so did his lordship, or

---

[227] *style*: see note 226.
[228] *under a force*: OED, *force sb.* I. 5. d. obs. under compulsion (*Ex.* 1387-1805).

any els that pleased. This opinion will in time wear out too, and they will come to the opinion wee have had some account of and mentioned to you, that you will be too cunning for all of 'em, and be a prey to none. This was upon your first removall. If ever, wee desturbe you in any thing that you positively determine concerning yourself farther then by telling you our thoughts of it, or refuse to assist you in your owne way all that in us lys, wee will give Lord [N.] leav to print what he comonly talks. You cannot imagine what a happyness wee have, and what a spirit it gives us, to know, as wee doe, that our endeavours are accepted and taken by you in good part. And of those, one hath bin, to shew to all, how much you are at your repose and eas, with your owne sister and where so that who pleaseth may be better informed that will, which some it seems have bin to the cost of 2 journeys. Sir T. says it is knowne who writes to you, and who you write to, and that one Mrs Sp. is the correspondent, whome I beleev he has visited, with spectacles upon his ears, and he reports that she says Sir T. doth not deserve you. But his name is not to be mentioned to her. He talks of the gallantry of D'an[vers] and what a brave proposition he made of giving you £10,000 and tho he has no great estate he has understanding to know how to keep that he has, but now he says he will desist, and give you no more trouble. He says still he will write to you and Lady D. says the same. Wee are clearly of opinion, there is nothing to be done to stop a fals fellow's mouth that will take the liberty of talking, but to deprive him of the occasion, and then he will leav of cours.[229] But the more they are pres't, the more and greater will the discours be, and now wee find the utmost of the pretensions,[230] and resolutions, which are not to gratifie you, or us, but to wait a better conjuncture to prevaile if possible. Wee thinck to trouble them no more, not expecting any advantage or information more then wee have, and it will but give occasion to them to invent discours, and magnifie their pretensions, becaus wee press them, more then they deserve. And in truth nothing can be done effectually. For an action at law for damages, is a mean cours, not used by persons of quality, (unless it be lords in scandala magnatum[231]) but by the meanest of the

---

[229] *of cours*: OED *a.* 36: as a matter of course (*Ex.* 1541-1862).

[230] *pretensions*: OED *sb.* 1. allegations or assertions, the truth of which is not proved or admitted (*Ex.* 1609-a. 1894).

[231] *in scandala magnatum*: (law Latin) (scandalum magnatum) 'words spoken in derogation of a peer, judge, or other great officer of the realm; which were subjected to peculiar punishments by a statute of Edward I, passed in 1275, and by divers other ancient statutes' (*Mozley and Whiteley*, p. 308).

people; and in truth doth alwais propagate scandall more then cure it; for all the towne usually assembles when such buissness stirrs. And as for actions in Doctors Comons[232] to be discharged[233] wee see plainely and the lord declares almost as much, that if you sued they will right downe fall upon your honour, and talk, and it may be swear, at least suggest in wrighting in the court, what to us and your freinds they have onely malitiously insinuated. Which tho never so fals will be an intollerable mischeif. [f. 1v] You must by all means press, Sir H.N.[234] - Now wee have received your last and to the business of Sir H.N's letter, since it cannot be had, let him have [his] humour, it is to no purpose farther to require it. If you had it you would see the repitition of what you have had with much addition. But there is no need of more information. All is now out. Wee now understand that Lady Dacres intends to write about your coming to towne and being of opinion that you may now scorne all things to that degree you master yourself and them. Wee doe not concurre with her in that perswasion; unless you had a double, at least an equall spirit, with hers; your education, nor temper is not that way, having most of the oblidging and complyant. The voyages of the ladys errant [to] Callis and Enfeild Chase,[235] are not to be forgotten, and there are such knights to

---

[232] *Doctors Comons*: Walker, *The Oxford Companion to Law*, p. 371, writes: 'About 1495 Richard Blodwell, Dean of the Arches, formed an Association of doctors of law and of the advocates of the Church of Christ at Canterbury, and it obtained premises in Paternoster Row, later known as Doctors' Commons. The Association was incorporated in 1768 as the College of Doctors of Law exercent in the Ecclesiastical and Admiralty Courts ... Doctors' Commons comprised all those licensed to practise as advocates before the courts, the principles and practice of which were founded on Roman law, which comprised the Court of Admiralty and the ecclesiastical courts with jurisdiction in matrimonial, testamentary, and probate matters. ... It was dissolved in 1858 after the society's exclusive rights to practise in the Admiralty and ecclesiastical courts had been abrogated.' See above, note 75, the passages from the manuscript volumes of Roger North's *Life of Dudley North* in which North claims that they feared Spencer would take action through the High Commission; see Introduction, pp. xxix-xxxi.

[233] *discharged*: OED v. II. 9. b. obs. cancelled, annulled (*Ex.* 1798-1885).

[234] *Sir H.N.*: i.e., Sir Henry North. The North brothers are asking Elizabeth to press Sir Henry for a copy of the letter Charles North wrote to him; see Document 26.

[235] *ladys errant... Callis and Enfeild Chase*: This might be a reference to Spencer's sisters' helping him in his suit. Callis is in Kent, near Broadstairs (i.e., east London) although Calais was often spelt this way in the seventeenth century. Enfield Chase is to the north of London, at this period, open country. It is not clear from the context why anyone should go to either place. The whole sentence here with its references to chivalry might be a veiled reference (again) to Butler's *Hudibras*, a poem of which Roger North was very fond. It is certainly

convoy others before they are ask't. This is our sence, expect securely,[236] new opportunitys may offer but nothing can intervene wherein you shall want the utmost assistance of
Your most affectionate humble servants
D. North M. North R⁰. North [each signs for himself]

Mr Soresby will write about sending the keys to get the writings of Sir Tho. Darcy's security which must be had becaus the mony is paying in. I have bin disappointed in securitys. And wee now want for Lely, North's and ourselves, but I have one for you next terme which I am assured will doe.

Document 44
'Lady Wiseman 14 December 1686'
[in Elizabeth Wiseman's hand]

[f. 2] Deare brothers,

I receiued a letter from the vnknown forsooth which pretends[237] to Neale, to advertize[238] me of the entregue betwixt them, and doe hope she will rest sattisfied with the account you gaue the embassidris which tis more then probable was the person agreived. I am sure he never had the least encouragement from me to vndertake such a foolish iorney but he resolu'd to take a denihall from none but my selfe, and confes'd, tho he was disheartn'd by all my friends, he resolu'd to make the attempt and had fixt his resolutions so, that he was vnalterable; I hope he will for the futur giue me no more trouble, tho I could not make him promise absolutly to disist. The lady sayes all is not gold that glysters and I am of the same oppinion, neither is it a hansome perriwig, a well sett cravet, gold wastcote with a coach and 6 shall tempt me to hazard the rest of my days in sorrow, nor the affliction I am now in shall make me marry any hobyhors of them all, so long as it pleases God to continu[e] me in my sences. I find Lord [N.] will never alter from his first principles: a friend to the villain and my

---

not a quotation from the poem although the line (with an addition) 'to Callis and [to] Enfield Chase' has the *Hudibras* metrical pattern.

[236] *expect securely*: wait confidently; rest assured. The sense of *expect* is that of *OED v.* I. *obs. intr.* to defer action until some contingency arises (*Ex.* 1560-1765). The sense of *securely* is that of *OED adv.* 1. *obs.* free from care, without misgiving (*Ex.* 1588-1802).

[237] *pretends*: *OED v.* II. 13. *b.* makes a suit for, tries to win in marriage (*Ex.* 1652-1874).

[238] *advertize*: *OED v.* 4. *trans. d.* to notify, inform (*Ex.* 1454-1850).

vtter enimye in it. I am sorry Munt [Mountague], as it hapen'd, I ever spoke of a noate under S.'s hand, because 'twill make them apprehend I think need requirs it and [that] he did it as from me, which I am so farr from that I defy the divill and all his works. Lett him do what he can, and when I come to town if he dares come neer me Ile spit in his beastly face. After that lett him take his course. I know so well my selfe and my behauour that I feare not the worst that he or his associates can be guilty of, lett them doe what they can. What the lord sayes is not at all to be valued so long as he acts quite contrary; and for my estate or person wheresoever I am I think my selfe sufficient to guard it from ever being in their power either civilly or otherwise, and my house a sanctuary. For nobody dares break open my doors, nor take a lady out of her coach in London streets, in the broad day light. Late I never stay out nor am alone (without it be Sunday eve) and tho I haue not the spirrit of some ladies (which shall be nameless)[239] yett I have mettle enough to know that for what I haue said or done yett I need not be asham'd to show my face or fly my countrey for such a blockhead as this is. I thank you for your good advise which shall allwayes be greatly esteem'd and follow'd by me as much as possibly I can, because I know you will councell me to nothing but what you know is for my advantage and sattisfaction and are so kind as to giue me leaue to deliver my owne sence. Whereas you mention the putting off my house in Soho Square: you know I took it for a yeare and if I would cannot part with it till the time be expir'd and would desire to know (supposing it were dischargd) where I shall place my goods, or if that be a place obnoxious,[240] what part else of the town you will think convenient for me to liue in. For according to the advise I haue formerly had from the deseased[241] I will never putt my selfe out of a house and home, and in order to that, he left me one and furniture whereby I might liue hapy. And I know my selfe so much in my own powr that I will not doe anything to make my life vneasy. The house at the [f. 1v] commons[242] is now in my hands and I think I am not like yett

---

[239] *some ladies (which shall be nameless)*: this is presumably a reference to her aunt, Lady Dacres.
[240] *obnoxious*: OED a. 1. exposed to harm (Ex. 1597-1891).
[241] i.e., her deceased husband, Sir Robert Wiseman.
[242] *house at the commons*: In British Library Add. MS 32510 (which contains chapters of an early version of Roger North's *Life of the Lord Keeper North*) f. 26v, Roger North describes his sister's living arrangements with Sir Robert Wiseman. They lived 'at the Comons, and afterwards at Chelsea'. Because Sir Robert Wiseman was Dean of the Arches he must have been one of the nineteen advocates required to rebuild Doctors' Commons after the Great Fire of 1666. It

to procure a tennant for it. If you aprove of that place better then the other I shall order my affairs accordingly, or if not, I desire to know how you would haue me dispos'd of. I know as I am a single woman I and my maid may bord anywhere, yet how will you dispose of my charge Mrs North[243] and her seruant. I doe assure you I know none of my relations will willingly be troubled with us: and besides I am one of those doe not loue to hang,[244] neither haue they houses to doe it. For tho I am extreamly well usd and civily treated as a guest yett were I fixt I must be burthensom. For when the Lady Wenyeue lies inn, the room I lodge in will be wanted; and tho perhaps she may complement me to her own enconvenience I will not strain the poynt. I look vpon the huff[245] of the Lord [North] before Lady Dacres to be a blast which will blow over, and a showing of his teeth where he has not pow'r to bite: neither shall he think he prevails so much vpon my weakness to make me feare any thing he can do, or alter my measurs[246] in the least for him[.] I think my selfe hapy (as you say) that I am out of the noyse[247] of them and so I resolue to keepe my selfe wherever I am. I haue not so many weomen relations left as to surround me; and doe not quesstion but through God's mercy, I may take

---

was in the part of London which now includes Queen Victoria Street and Upper Thames Street. See Squibb, G.D. (1977), pp. 67-71.

[243] *Mrs North*: It is not clear who this is. Two candidates are possible. The first is one of the sisters of Robert North, a distant cousin, who is discussed in North, Roger (1995), pp. 187-9. He had several sisters, some of whom apparently married; but it is possible that an unmarried sister lived with Elizabeth Wiseman, a practice of family benevolence which seems to have been common (at least in the North family). Robert North and his sisters are described by Roger North as having been left in very straitened circumstances. The second is Elizabeth's niece, the daughter of the deceased Lord Keeper, Sir Francis North. When his wife died in 1678 Sir Francis sent his only surviving daughter, Anne, then three years old, to live with Elizabeth Wiseman. In his *Life of the Lord Keeper*, Roger North says that Elizabeth was then living 'at Chelsea, where also was a good school for yong ladys of quallity, which was an advantag': see North, Roger (1995), p. 217. In 1686 Anne would have been eleven. She might have been boarding at school, or she might be the Mrs North referred to here. Certainly, Elizabeth's referring to Mrs North as her 'charge' suggests that it is a younger person she is referrring to.

[244] *to hang*: OED v. II. intr. 14. e. attach oneself as a dependant or parasite; to be a hanger-on (*Ex.* 1535-1832). Here also with the meaning of 1. i. to be burdensome.

[245] *huff*: OED sb. 2. b. fit of petulance caused by an affront, real or supposed (*Ex.* 1684-1869).

[246] *alter my measurs*: OED, measure sb. IV. 21. a plan or course of action; *measures obs.* as in *to break (a person's) measures*: to frustrate his plans (*Ex.* 1698-1899). So here, 'change my plans'.

[247] *noyse*: OED 2. *obs.* slander, scandal (*Ex.* 1297-1734).

sufficient care to preserue my selfe from any villianys that can be attempted. It seems it is still conceiu'd I am vnder a force,[248] and all the world will never convince them of that erronious oppinion so long as I absent my selfe from home. That I hate S., time will sufficiently proue and I hope it will be neuer the less said I am too cunning for them and will be a prey to none tho I disert not my habitation and fly not my countrey for such a rascall which I look vpon to be more disreputeation[249] then any thing is in his pow'r to doe. Neither doe I find the bussines the least better then when I was there nor will it be if I stay this seven years. The sparks are of the mind I will marry. I never de[c]lared my selfe of that opinion yett nor shall they find it so. But lett them say what pleases them I reguard it not: but they shall never find my discourse or actions tending that way. Sir Theo. sayes 'tis known who I write to. I doe not at all desire to keepe it secrett nor doe I care who sees those letters being only of course[250] and civility, nor shall he ever improue his knowledg in my affairs by conversing with them. He is no doubt a spy for Danvers and giues him intelligence of all he sees or hears, for when Danvers was here he told me such and such things were certainly true for he had them by those that had it from Mr Roger North's own mouth - speaking of my place of abode, and he has never writt me yett but if he does I know how to guard my selfe and what to beleiuve of his twattle. [f. 1] I am of your mind, it will not be well for me to commence a sute to gett cleare of this fellow for the reasons you mention. If he begin lett him. I question not but we shall be prepared to answere, and he will advantage himself by it full as much as Sir Richard Wyseman did in the case of Winter, procur'd ignominy and shame and so desisted. What they can sweare I feare not, neither will it be at all credited from such wittnesses (tho I hope it will never come to it). My Lady Dacres you say designs me a letter about my return which I shall not in the least think of till after Chris-mas, if you think it convenient then, for I rely so much vpon your better iudgments that I cannot speak possitiuely to any thing, because I am assurd you will order all things for the best, and for my advantage. I beleiue you will now alter your oppinion and thinke us weomen as impertinent with our pens as v[s]uall[y] our tongus are, but if mine has now exceeded, I ask pardon. But you haue brought it

---

[248] *vnder a force*: see note 228.
[249] *disreputeation*: OED obs. 1. privation or loss of reputation; dishonour, disgrace (*Ex*. 1601-1874).
[250] *of course*: OED, *course sb*. III. 19. custom, practice (*Ex. c*. 1325-1886). She means that her letters deal only with customary and ordinary matters.

vpon your selues by giueing lyberty, for out of the abundance of my heart my mouth speaks. But after all I am at your seruice. I haue sent the key of my cabinett to Mr Soresbie with direction where he may haue Sir Tho. Daveys' writings. It will be a great obligement[251] (as you know who sayes) if you can procure a security for the mony. I haue not further to trouble you with, but seruices from and to etc., and remain as ever bound
    Your most really affectionate sister
    and humble seruant
Brettnam December the 14th '86   Elizabeth Wyseman

Document 45
Letter from Dudley North, Mountague North and Roger North to Elizabeth Wiseman [14] December 1686
[in Roger North's hand]

[f. 1] Dearest sister,

Wee have reflected since wrighting our last that it may be that you may thinck what wee said concerning your not living independently by yourself, that is, disposing your hous, which is a standing charg, and may be resumed at any time, and forming yourself to a different cours of life, to be alwais in a circle of weomen relations, might be precipitate, and proceeding from the frett[252] of the present conjuncture of your affaires. But to be very plaine which is the present, and shall be our future, porpose, wee must needs say wee have considered it as a convenience to you severall years, even from your first beginning of setling yourself, which you may remember by divers instances of discourses, and proposalls that have past. But your mind was rather to be by your self, and wee cannot say but it was rationall enough, abstracted from the impudent obtrusions of fals and base designing people, which wee foresaw, but you were not so much aware of. It is almost impossible for a lady to steer her self cleer of towne talk, which is allways bad, or ruine in such circumstances. Nothing but the spirit of Lady Da., which is to be feared, never reigned in our tribe, could support 20 years as she did in towne; but even in her case, it is to be considered she was no booty to any, as you are, for she had but a joynture of £800 per annum, and with that she fell in

---

[251] *obligement*: OED sb. 2. obligation (moral or legal); a kindness, favour (*Ex.* 1611-1828).
[252] *frett*: OED sb. 3. vexation (*Ex.* 1556-1885).

a ditch at last.²⁵³ And if it were possible for you to support such a bravery, as should make anyone tremble that comes in your way, it is possible you might enjoy some tollerable quiet, with the exercise of a greater ill nature, and that continually, then you are acquainted with, or in any sort used to. But civility and temper²⁵⁴ which are your vertues, in these affaires are destruction, and produce troubles of which you are not without experience. And after all nothing that is acceptable is troublesome or unreasonable. Whatever comes in that garb is fals, and treacherous. The good finds its fellow out, and the sooner by keeping out of the nois of such trumpery, that frights all that is valuable. But the end of this is onely to introduce what was hinted before that you must judg and determine your owne conduct; wee doe neither desire, nor pretend²⁵⁵ to sway you, in any thing against your owne perswasion; nor would wee have you have the least thought or imagination, that wee should take it ill if you are of an opinion different; for it is your right, and in your power, and God forbid but you should have the utmost scope, in things that concerne onely yourself. But wee shall whatever you doe or choos find us in the same air,²⁵⁶ and easyness as ever, and never faile to contribute our outmoust endeavours, both to assist, and entertein you, as formerly. Next to

---

[253] North, Roger (1995), p. 34, writes of the legal work his brother Francis (the Lord Keeper) did for their aunt:
  The Lady Dacres had suits depending against [Chaloner] Chute, the eldest son of her husband [i.e., her second husband, Chaloner Chute] then deceast, for a sum of mony secured upon land by her marriage contract; which Chute had marryed her daughter [Catherine Lennard] and dying left upon her hands 4 grand children to take care of. She entered upon the estate, and took the profits for divers years, by which she became accountable. His Lordship [i.e., Francis North who was acting for her] was sensible that his aunt ran great hazards of being called to an account by the eldest son [i.e., her eldest grandson, also Chaloner] at his full age, and instead of having her dett, be made a dettor, advised her to get a decree, and a manager appointed and she to answer onely, what monys she actually received, and as things fell out afterwards the reasons for this precaution appeared most lively, for it preserved her (who kept no good account) from orall testimony of imaginary values, which had pinched her to the quick if she had not had that defence.
See also *Mr. Chute's Case upon the Lady Dacre's Appeal*, London, 1685; *Mr. Chute's Case upon the Matter*, London, ?1681; *Mr. Chute's Petition of Appeal*, London, 1685.
[254] *temper*: OED sb. I. 3. mental balance and composure; command over the emotions, esp. anger; equanimity (*Ex.* 1603-1878).
[255] *pretend*: OED v. I. 9. venture, presume (*Ex.* 1482-1869).
[256] *air*: OED sb. III. 14. b. obs. disposition, mood (*Ex.* 1655-1728).

our service to you, our [f. 1v] ayme is to have the satisfaction that wee have bin as free with you as with our owne souls. And for that reason must importune you not to reckon our opinion any incumbrance, but to act according to your owne judgment; and if wee hint any thing to you that may give you information leading to your owne advantage wee have our executors. And persuant to this wee thinck fit to add, that at this time, you are more the discours of the towne then you have bin at any time yet, becaus upon Lady Da.'s arivall, and conversing with severall of the discoursive part of the femalle towne, has set a new ferment to work, but much to your advantage. For lady St Johns,[257] who is a neer relation of Sp.'s and my lady's frequent companion, doth detest her kindsman; and on Tewsday last I waited on her, and found Lord Sussex[258] there, who, as she told me, informed her that the Lord S[underland] did declaime against the same for doing things so unworthy a gentleman, as threatning and persuing a lady at this rate was. And besides the stratagems of the sharks which are infinite, and unknowne; if you were in towne, you would have all gossiping impertinent, and buisy, bantering sort of ladys come to you in the guise of freindship and acquaintance, as in ordina[ry] visits. And they would be pumping, sifting, and provoking you to talk, and defend your self upon particulars, and provoke you by telling you what others say'd, and take advantage of your discourses, and words to make sport in the next company they come in, and so send one and other, as beggars and trumpetters doe. And it is impossible for the cunningest creature in nature to defend against this humour[259] any other way, then by avoiding, to give that advantage. Therefore it may now come in as a generall caution to you scarce ever to be forgot, that when you are discours't with upon this affair, or ask't any thing tending to it, to say nothing of circumstance[260] about it. For that will alwais give occasion [to] imagine more then you say, speak as cautiously and complacently as you will, for people judg not so much by words as by things which they will understand directly opposite to the expression of them. But to defye the villane, and all his works, to call him lyar, base fellow, no gentleman; that you could not have

---

[257] *Lady St Johns*: This is probably Joanna, eldest daughter of Lord Chief Justice Oliver St John (d. 1673) who married Sir Walter St John of Lydiard-Tregoze in Wiltshire.

[258] *Lord Sussex*: i.e., Thomas Lennard, created Earl of Sussex from 1674, and related to Lady Dacres's first husband, Lord Dacres.

[259] *humour*: OED sb. II. mental quality or condition (Ex. 1590-1863); here, a disposition to gossip.

[260] *circumstance*: OED sb. II. 7. b. obs. importance, moment (Ex. 1586-1676).

imagined there had bin so much baseness in the world as there is, and such like, still declining the discours, and not touching it without generall resentments, and no more. Since the writing of this wee received youre from whence wee are glad to find such a bon courage[261] as you shew, which in good earnest is one very considerable peice of armour. But in the maine wee [f. 2] expected that you would have those sentiments you express. Wee have already say'd what is proper in answer, which is in short that your owne heart is your guid, and you have reason to move in your owne best approved methods, wee hoping you will find all content, soe much the more by your hearty swaggering. Wee have conferred with Lady Dacres upon this affair, and as wee beleeve she hath expressed in her letter she is for your returne to London, in full storme against all villanes that should thinck to deprive any person of her liberty, and by the grace of God, in her case they should not doe it. But she is most positive that wherever you are you must not be alone, that is without weomen company. Therefore you must needs take care of yourself in that and provide some company against[262] you come. And wee are also clearly of her mind in it. The Lord — doth blare as bad or wors then ever declaring all to be done at your desire, and the journey to T[ooting] to be an assignation of your making. Before this passage, which wee had from Lady D. his lordship did solemnly declare that some great thing wors then what has hapned to you may fall out in a fortnight, and if it doth he is not to be blamed, becaus he would use all his endeavour to stifle it. What he means wee know not, having not the guift of conjuring, but suppose it may be the graine[263] of his genius[264] which useth not to be very regardable.[265] Time will try. This is very remarkable, that Lady N. hath not spoke one word to Lady D. of this buissnes, and Lady D. is too proud to begin with her, and says truly she scornes it, and doth not like their ways so well to promote the discours. Whether it would have bin better or not if you had bin here, wee being no profets, cannot tell, but in all probability it would have bin wors, tho in what kind is unknowne. The time of this Xmas may be very considerable for information. Wee shall have the advantage of your company whenever you are here, the want of which wee have lamented most extreamly. It is to no porpose to say any thing

---

[261] *bon courage*: (French) good heart, cheerful spirits.

[262] *against*: OED prep. B. 18. by the time that (*Ex. c.* 1300-1848).

[263] *graine*: OED sb. IV. 16. *fig.* quality, temper, inclination (*Ex.* 1641-1884).

[264] *genius*: OED sb. 3. *a. obs.* disposition (*Ex.* 1581-1804).

[265] *regardable*: OED *a. obs.* worthy of notice, noticeable (*Ex.* 1591-1785).

to the questions you ask about your changing your cours of life becaus you have oblidged us with the making knowne your owne opinion with which wee shall alwais comply. After supper and claret, hath made nonsence and blotting which you must excuse from

    Your most affectionate humble servants and brothers

    D. North M. North R⁰. North [each signs for himself]

There is a project going with Lady D. about the Lord Hollis,[266] of whome you may have an account from Mrs Mascall if you thinck fitt to inquire.

Document 46
Letter from Elizabeth Wiseman 21 December 1686
[in Elizabeth Wiseman's hand]

[Addressed: 'These to the Honourable Mr North at his chambers in the Middle Temple London']
[f. 2]   Dec. the 21th [sic] '86
Deare Brothers,

I receiued not yours till late this evening so must desire you'l accept of a short epistle. I thought we should have faild of our entelligence and correspondence quite this week, for on Sunday when we came from church bigg with the exspectation of our letters [we] were mett with the sadd accident of our carrier's haueing been robb'd, our letters stamped into the dirt by the rogues, the goods all seiz'd, carrier cutt and hak't most misserably, and lost a consid[e]rable summ of mony, and being in years[267] and vnder these afflictions was forst to lie by the way not able to reach home. Here amongst us the lammentation of our Lady Jane and the burning of mother Low;[268] Sir George had sent for a new beaux hatt to make his worship fine against Xmas that was without doubt vpon some of the villians heads, Lady Wenyeve sent for lace to make her ladyship fine against lieing inn, Lady W. severall things from the Exchange,[269] all which no doubt were gone to

---

[266] *Lord Hollis*: i.e., Francis Holles, Baron Holles of Ifield (1627-90) son of Sir Denzil Holles.
[267] *in years*: OED year sb. 5. b. old, aged (Ex. 1569-1868).
[268] *lammentation of our Lady Jane ... mother Low*: It is not clear what this refers to: perhaps a popular song or a ballad?
[269] *the Exchange*: This was the New Exchange, built in 1608-9 in the Strand, London. It was popular after the Restoration and particularly after the Great Fire

make their bagages fine. So that here was such a lammentation, and consultation about drawing vp a breife, to make a gathering as you never heard. And we did not at all quesstion, but that we should haue great releife from the Brethren.[270] But at last (as I said,) we received our goods, but such a parcell of letters as was never seen so dirty and wett that we could scarce part, or open without tearing all to peices. I thank you most kindly for yours with the good advice which [I] shall endeauour to follow allwayes and as for the lord's blaring and stareing, shall feare him not but will keepe my selfe altogether out of his way, and his like - The assignation to Too[ting] is like all the rest, and as little to [f. 1v] be minded. What great things this next fortnight shall produce, we shall exspect,[271] but doe hope nothing exstraordinary will hapen ill on my side, and if you all be safe I feare nothing. Tis thought the lord designs to be at his seat[272] this Xmas, and perhaps thincks of comming hether which if [he] does, shall faile in his exspectation of seeing me. At my return to London which [I] suppose may be convenient after the hollidayes, I will be sure to sett a guard vpon my selfe, especially the tongue, as well before prattleing weomen as others for I am very much of your mind, that they will make their vissits principally, vpon the humour[273] of entregue. But I will be sure to take care and order my selfe accordingly, with a defyance of all villiany. We had some little glimps of hope that we might see some of you here this good time, which if you be so good natur'd will be a sattisfaction beyond exspression, especially to me. I receiued a letter from my Lady Dacres to the same effect you wrote. I haue return'd her my thanks in short, for I am very iealous[274] in talking much, to a ladie of her spiritt which may make it worss, and will leaue her to muse vpon what she knows allready. I fancy the Lady N. begins to be asham'd of what is done and will not discourse [with] Lady Da. for feare of being worsted at her own weapon.[275] Lett me now beg you will excuse this

---

of 1666 when it took over some of the business of the Royal Exchange. It was an imposing building with galleries inside along which were many shops, mainly drapers and mercers.

[270] *releife from the Brethren*: I do not know what (or whom) Elizabeth refers to here.

[271] *exspect*: OED v. I. 2. trans. obs. to wait for, await (*Ex.* 1585-1822).

[272] *his seat*: i.e., at Kirtling (or Catledge).

[273] *humour*: OED sb. II. 6. *b*. inclination or disposition for an action; a fancy (to do something) (*Ex.* 1590-1863).

[274] *iealous*: OED a. 6. suspiciously vigilant (*Ex.* 1601-1866).

[275] *worsted at her own weapon*: OED v. 2. *b. trans.* defeated (in argument) (*Ex.* 1636-1902); here the point is that Lady North is fearful of being out-argued by

scratching for I am forst to write very late, and accept of my hearty wishes to you all a merry Xmass, as also to the good Lady D. North and that she will give her pretty son Dud[l]y a treble blessing from me. Seruice etc., to etc.

[f. 1] We often remember you in our cupps, and I never drink clarrett but to your healths for the continuance of which is the hearty prayer of

> Your most really affectionate
> sister and humble seruant
> Elizabeth Wizeman

Pray tell Munt [Mountague] I haue had a very seveare letter from Lady Russell because he, and I, did not waite attop[276] of her ladyship when we lay at Bury. He must look to take vp the bussiness when he sees her next.

Document 47
'Mr White Dec. 29 [i.e. 26] 1686'
[in Francis White's hand]

[Addressed: 'For the Honourable Mr Roger North']
[f. 1]   Dec. 26 '86
Sir,

Wer I capable of wrighting a romance you should haue it in all its parts: but I humbly desyre you to take truth as I can tell it. Once vpon a tyme Dame Spycer received a let[t]er from her vnfortunate son Philander, that hee was now wean'd from his amoures and that if a woman had the face of an angell with the wealth of both Indiæs hee could not love, hee would not mar[r]y: and indeed after a heroe has layd siedge to six faire fortreses to be forsed to ryse and march of[f]; it must needs be great mat[t]er of mo[r]tification. But this is not all the worst, for Gran[n]y sayes her son having plyghted his fayths and troath hee cannot now if hee would mar[r]y any other and tis her opinione the widow is in the same predicament. But there is a certaine atorny has spoke bugg[277] words against the family of the Spycers: saying they were all poor and not worth a

---

Lady Dacres whom she regards as more fierce in wielding words than she is.
[276] *attop*: Elizabeth has deleted 'vpon' before this word which is the sense here, although the *OED* gives 'atop' only in the sense of physically being on top of.
[277] *bugg*: *OED a. obs.* proud, conceited, fine (*Ex.* 1567-1881).

groat, which the head of the family [h]as bin aquainted with and has promis'd to remember.

I haue gon as far as I can at present in the busines of Shaftswell Mr Wyet and his father in law haue promist that you shall haue the first of[f]er. They demand £1700 and part of the mony to remaine in your hands at £5 per cent:

I am Sir
Your most faithfull and most humble servant
Fra: White[278]

Document 48
'Oxenbridges Note 7 Apr. 1687'
[in Clement Oxenbridge's hand]

[f. 1] I perfectly well remember that in the latter end of November and December last, Mr Spencer much courted mee to bring him to wait on Mrs Susan Goodwin in order to mariage pretending[279] hee had £1200 per annum in possession and £2000 per annum in revercion, and could bee made a baron or any other honor, shee should desire, by the meanes of the Lord Sonderland his neere relacion. Whereupon I brought him twice to her, at her owne lodging where hee had free discource with her, and afterwards went alone and vrged to bee accepted as her servant and husband. I also went with him to her lodging often, when shee was abroad, hee still discourcing mee on the termes, hee was ready to proceed on to let her dispose of her estate, as shee pleas'd, if they should have noe children, promising mee a noble requitall for my civillity herein. But shee having inquird and found his estate but £500 per annum totally declind the proposition. And all this I can make oath, when requird.
7th Aprill, 1687.   Clem Oxenbridge

---

[278] *Francis White*: He was the steward at Wroxton, the home of the deceased Lord Keeper North. Both Roger and Dudley, as the Lord Keeper's executors, often spent time at Wroxton. Since Wroxton is close to Hanwell, Francis White would have been in a good position to hear all the Spencer gossip.
[279] *pretending*: OED v. I. 7. alleging (falsely) (*Ex.* 1610-1839).

Documents 49 and 50
Letter to the Earl of Yarmouth from Charles North 3 May 1687
[in Charles North's hand: copy in Elizabeth Paston's hand]

[Elizabeth Wiseman has now married the Earl of Yarmouth, William Paston. The original of this letter, in Charles North's hand, is very fragile and the paper fragmentary. It is addressed: 'These to the right Honourable Earle of Yarmouth and Controller of his Majesty's houshold present'. The following is a transcription of Lady Yarmouth's copy.]

[f. 2] My Lord

Your lordship desireing it vnder my hand as I said before, this is humbly to certifie that I never knew any thing of contract passing between my sister now happily your Lady and Mr Spencer and that if he has putt in any libell to that effect I am wholly a strainger to it and am farr from ever hearing any such words that way. The forward gentleman was in my house saying I Robert take thee Eliz. but I stop't his carrier and said matters were not come to that. My sister was so farr from saying so that I haue heard her severall times spake to me that matters should not goe on between them which I (who I confess was friend to that match before she had the honour of being addressed to by your lordship) did reconcile well as I could but in any indirect way never, and I know nothing of any vnhandsome carriage towards her from him more then a kiss at the balcony at Tooting which I thought too publicque for one so little while a pretender to her. Ile [f. 2v] assure your Lordship my honour is too deare to suffer any vilanous affront to be done my sister and am ready and alwayes was to testifie in any court whatsoever that I never knew any thing like a contract nor tending that way from her to him, and much less any wayes misbecoming her birth, she haueing alwayes behaueed her selfe so without any blott or scandall that it must needs be a scandelous and vilianous procecution that defames her for any misbehauour in poynt of honour. This my lord I was allwayes ready to giue vnder [my] hand it being the very truth which with my affectionate seruice to your lady concludes this of May the 3rd
   from
   Your lordship's most humble seruant
   North and Grey

I am so farr from encouraging this way of proceeding that I haue alwayes discouraged it to my vttmost and will while I am in being and who soever dares to say the contrary wrongs me and this I am ready to demonstrate in any way I shall be required.

Document 51
'The passage at Lord Yarmouth's with Lord North' 8 May 1687
[in Roger North's hand]

8 May. 1687.
[f. 1] At my Lord Yarmouth's hous, the Lord North being there, with the Lord Y. and Ro[ger] North and Robt. Foley onely more in company the Lord North affirmed (among much other discours) the matter of his last letter that he knew nothing of contract that past at any time between Spencer, and his sister. And this was upon his being pres't by the Lord Yarmouth that Sp. had in his libel pretended[280] that he and his wife were his onely wittnesses. And his lordship farther prest him to say what his wife had declared upon that matter, and he say'd expresly that his wife had declared to him that she knew nothing of any such contract; whereupon the lord desired us to observe which wee did. Wee thinck, upon my Lord Yarmouth's repeating the question he said the same thing againe. But Robert Foley then repeated the words to him againe, he being advised of our caution in order to testifie (as wee thinck) did begin to shufle, and depart from the express words, and say'd, Nothing that she thought a contract, and being farther prest upon the words, said he would, or could not answer for her knowledg.

R^o. North
Robt. Foley [each signs for himself]

Document 52
'Sir H. Beddingfeild[281] May[282] 1687'
[in Henry Beddingfield's hand]

[Addressed: 'For the Earle of Yarmouth']
[f. 1] My Lord
I haue been this morning with my Lord North at Mr Spencer's chamber and after many words too long for this paper wee cam[e] to this point, that a generall discharge for all sutes and demands shalbbee on either syde signed and sealed which left in my hands shall bee deliuered at my being present att Doctors Comons. After

---

[280] *pretended*: OED vb. 4. b. obs. professed, claimed (*Ex.* 1427-1784).
[281] *Sir H. Beddingfeild*: Sir Henry Beddingfield was Lord Chief Justice of the Common Pleas, 1686-7. In North, Roger (1995) he is described as someone of whom Francis North had a high opinion.
[282] The date in May must be one of the following Mondays: 16, 23, or 30.

Mr Spencer shall withdraw his claime, in such manner as the court shall require to render all claimes of that kind fruittless hereafter to bee putt in by him. T. Paston and Rawlens[283] are included in the peace, both partyes to paye their respectiue charges, sessations of assaults and batteryes from this moment. What happened this morning by 2 onknowne persons was carried to my Lord Sunderland and my Lady Peterborrow[284] which will I feare make some knaves. You are desyred to speake to Mr Roger North to draw up the releases for your lordshipp to signe to Spencer, and for Spencer to signe to your lordshipp including Captain Thomas Rawlens. Pray lett the foule drafts[285] be sent me that I may show it Mr Spencer and vpon his approbation gett them sealed and then finish all which I judge not improper to accelarate. I hope I haue acted not to your preiudice,
    I am
    Your Lordshipps humble servant
    Henry Bedingfeld
London
Monday

Document 53
'Bond of Mr Spencer to the E. of Y'

[f. 1] Noverint universi per presentes me Robertum Spencer de London arma teneri et firmiter obligari pronobili ?et vitto comiti Yarmouth in decem mille librar[i] bone et legalii monetae angliae solvedi eidem ?et vitto comiti Yarmouth aut suo cert- attornat- executor- vel administrator siue ad quam quidem solutionem bene et fideliter faciendum obligo me heredes executores et adm: meos firmiter per presentes sigillo meo sigillat dat.
    ann Regni Dominu ...
Jacobi secundi dei gratia Angliae Scotiae Franciae et Hibernae Regis fedei defensoris etc. tertio annoque Domini 1687

---

[283] T. Paston is the Earl of Yarmouth's brother, Thomas, referred to in Document 57 as 'my brother captain'. Rawlens is also referred to as Captain Thomas Rawlens in the present Document. In Document 57 he is preferred to Thomas Paston for making enquiries about the genuineness of Spencer's challenge.
[284] *my Lady Peterborrow*: i.e., Penelope, wife of Henry Mordaunt, Earl of Peterborough, a convert to the Church of Rome in 1686. Penelope was the daughter of Barnabas O'Brien, Earl of Thomond.
[285] *foule drafts: foule* OED ad. A. II. 3. obs. first (of the copy of a writing) defaced with corrections (*Ex.* 1467-1888).

The condition of this obligation is such that in case the aboue bounden Robert Spencer, doe not make, enter, sue forth or prosecute any appeale or suite of appeale unto the king's majestie his comissioners or delegates any or either of them, in any ecclesiastical courte, the courte of Chancery, or before the lord chancellor, or elsewhere within the kingdome of England; from or against any award sentence or decree; now made or pronounct or to be at any time hereafter made or pronounct by Sir Thomas Exton[286] of Doctors Comons knight or his surrogate or deputy in a certaine cause now or lately depending before him or them, at the suite or prosecution of the said Robert Spencer against the Right Honourable Elizabeth the now wife of the said Right Honourable William Earle of Yarmouth and some time since the widdow and relict of Sir Robert Wiseman deceast, upon pretence of contract or otherwise; then this obligation to be voyd and of none effect, otherwise to remaine and be in full force and vertue

Seald and Delivered
in the presence of

Document 54
'Sp[encer]'s Releas to Mr P. and Mr R.' [1687]
[in legal hand]

[f. 1] Know all men by these presents that I Robert Spencer of London esquire haue remisd released and for euer quitt clayme, and by these presents doe remise release and for euer quittt claym unto the Honourable Thomas Paston brother of the right Honourable William Earle of Yarmouth and . . . [sic] Rawlins of . . . . [sic] and euery of them theire and euery of theire heires executors and administrators all and all manner of action and actions cause and causes of action suites bills bonds writings obligatory debts dues dutys accounts summe and summes of money judgments executions extents quarrells, controversies trespasses damages and demands whatsoeuer both in law and equity or otherwise howsoeuer, which against the said Thomas Paston and . . . . Rawlins or either of them I euer had and which I my heires executors or administrators shall or may haue clayme or demand for or by reason or meanes of any matter cause or thing

---

[286] *Sir Thomas Exton*: He was Chancellor of the diocese of London (1663-85) and appointed Dean of the Arches and judge of the Admiralty in 1686. He died on 4 November 1688.

whatsoeuer from the beginning of the world to the day of the date of these presents and I doe hereby declare and signifye my desire and intent that all and euery indictment and indictments information and informations preferred[287] or exhibited, or which shall or may hereafter be preferred or exhibited at the king's suite for any matter cause or thing whatsoeuer already past relating to me or upon my relation or prosecution, doe cease and be noe farther prosecuted, and that nolle prosequis[288] be entered thereupon accordingly in wittness whereof I haue hereunto sett my hand and seale this ... [blank] day of ... [blank] annoque Domini 1687
Sealed and delivered in the presence

Document 55
'Sir H. Beddingfeild 16 June 1687'
[In Sir Henry Beddingfield's hand]

[Addressed: 'For Roger North esq.']
[f. 1] Sir,

I was with Mr Spencer who approves of the release but his friends and councell tells him that vnless my Ladye Yarmouth giues the same under her hand he can be noe wayes safe; for in case my Lord dyes, she may call him to account. This he euer told my Lord North and he seemes positiue in itt. It appeares but reasonable, though you are the better judge, and I
    Your humble servant
    Henry Bedingfeld
Thursdaye morning

[on the verso of the leaf, in Roger North's hand:]

               30. June. 1687
Sir H. B. discoursing with Mr S. he took occasion to say, he had wittnesses of the contract and tho my Lord N. say[s] he hear[d] non yet he saw her lips goe.

---

[287] *preferred*: *OED v.* II. 5. laid before someone formally for consideration (*Ex.* 1559-1885).

[288] *nolle prosequis*: = *nolle prosequi* (law Latin) *lit.* to be unwilling to prosecute. This 'was a formal averment by the plaintiff in an action, that he would not further prosecute his suit as to one or more of the defendants, or as to part of the claim or cause of action. Its effect was to withdraw the cause of an action, in respect of which it was entered, from the record' (*Mozeley and Whiteley*, p. 220).

Document 56
Letter to the Earl of Yarmouth from Robert Spencer 7 January 1689: date described by Roger North as 7 December 1689
[in Robert Spencer's hand]

[Addressed: 'These for the Right Honourable the earle of Yarmouth neare Norwich in Norfolk']
[f. 1]   January the 7th 1689
My Lord,

I have suffer'd extreamly vpon your lordship's account, and so much that I find it an obiection to my preferment, for not revenging it sooner. Therefore my lord I must now demand satisfaction of you, for my wrongs and therefore I desire you will name tyme and place, and I will meet you. I thinke Newmarkett no ill place since it is halfeway and I will post my selfe at Cattellidge, ready to hear from you, but I will attend your answere in town which I desire may be directed for me at Man's Coffee House near Cherring Crosse[289] and pray lett it be next post. As for your brother[290] that pretends[291] to have affronted me, I have declard him a rasscall and lyer to all the world [f. 1v] and if he be that bulley you belive him let him vindicate himselfe and give him notis of it, and that I say he is rather a villenous assassinate, that would take a barbarous addvantage to murther a man, then doe a hansom action. As for your brother Roger, he has bin all ready chastis'd for his saucy talking in missrepresenting me vnder an odious carecter. I shall bring a friend with me, and I desire you to doe the same. So expecteing to hear from you by the first, I have nothing more to add I am
    My Lord
    Your Lordship's servant
    Robert Spencer

---

[289] *Man's Coffee House near Cherring Crosse*: Lillywhite, Byrant (1963) p. 83 says that this coffee house, established in 1666 by Alexander Man, was also called 'The Royal Coffee House' and 'The Golden Fleece'.
[290] *your brother*: i.e., Captain Thomas Paston.
[291] *pretends*: OED v. I. 9. presumes (*Ex.* 1482-1869).

Document 57
'Lord Yarmouth, Jan. 1689'
[in the Earl of Yarmouth's hand]

[Addressed: 'These for the honorable Roger North esq. at his house in the Piaches in Covent Garden London']
[f. 1]   Jan ye 13th '89
Deare Brother,

I ask your pardon for not sooner thanking you for your last letter. Christmas time must plead my excuse. I send you two letters inclosed which I desire you not to be surprized at it being a sham as I judge of Mr Seccomb's as you may see by the letter he sent me 10 days [ago] which compared to be the same writing he was sent formerly by my Lady North and is as full of tricks and rogueries as any man. I did once promise him something in being assistant in a matter before I had the happynesse of knowing you or your family and this I judge is some trick of hisn [sic] to be instrumentall in making up a quarrell as he will call it and will take the letter perhapps at the coffee house if I should send one or make a May game of it with my Lady North. Howsoever they must not think to scare me. Something must be done with as little notice as is convenient else twill make them think I am afraid and attempt something they never durst so I desire you seriously to consider what is left to be done. I was unwilling to acquaint my brother captain who would make too great a noise of it. Therefore I think you would do well to gett Mr Rawlings to go to Mans Coffee house at Charring Crosse immediately upon the receipt of this and inquire for this Spencer and know whether he wrote any such letter and whether he be in town [f. 1v] and what he say to it. For if they should be in good earnest I must speak with your friend at Catlidge and both shall haue their bellysfull[.] I hope and accordingly shall take my measures but naming no lodging and the hands compared being exactly the same and I question not but tis a shamm. However some inquiry must be made else the cowards will grow bold and Rawlings is the fittest person you can imploy. He lives at the upper end of Swallow Street on the back side of the house my lady Harvy dwelt in. Desire him to be very private in the matter. Excuse my giving you this trouble being most heartily
    Your affexionate brother
    Yarmouth
My service to my brother and sister Dudly's.

[This is the last surviving document in the series. We do not know whether Spencer had 'satisfaction' or not. Little more is recorded of the Earl of Yarmouth and even less of his wife, Elizabeth. The North family kept no more of her letters. Some account of the earl is made under the chapter heading 'The End of the Pastons' in Ketton-Cremer, R.W. (1944), *Norfolk Portraits*, pp. 22-57. His first wife died in July 1684, leaving three sons and two daughters, none of whom survived him nor had issue who survived but who were all alive when Paston married Elizabeth Wiseman. William Paston was interested, like his father, in alchemy, and was a speculator in a copper mine in America and a lead mine in Wales. Like Roger North, he was a non-juror, refusing to take the oath of allegiance to William and Mary after the revolution of 1688-9: he was one of the few peers who refused to do so. Ketton-Cremer has this to say of him and Elizabeth, his wife:

> As a known and open partisan of James, his conduct was closely watched; and in the summer of 1690, when William was fighting James in Ireland, and an invasion from France was hourly expected, he was committed to the Tower.[292] ... Lady Yarmouth petitioned the Queen to lodge with him, and was allowed to enter the Tower 'on condition that she and her maid do not go abroad, and, in case they do, they are not to be permitted to return to him'. He was released when the danger blew over; but during the next invasion alarm in 1692, which was ended by the battle of La Hogue, he was committed to the Tower again.

Ketton-Cremer also says that by 1708 Paston had 'vast debts'. When he died in 1632, two years after his wife's death, he was declared bankrupt. Nothing is known of Elizabeth after her marriage beyond her support of her husband by wishing to join him in the Tower.

---

[292] Ketton-Cremer refers to a letter from Roger North in which he claimed that 'There is no charge against him, and this is done for security in dangerous times.' The reference is in a letter to his niece, Anne Foley, daughter of his sister Anne, dated 7th July, 1690. The letter is reprinted in *The Lives of the Norths*, vol. 3 pp. 224-5. The passage, in post script, begins 'Lord Yarmouth is committed to the Tower for high treason and not allowed bail.'

Bibliography

Alumni Oxonienses: the members of the University of Oxford 1500-1714 (1892), vol. 4, Oxford University Press, Oxford and London.

Astell, Mary (1730, 1970), *Some Reflections Upon Marriage*, 4th edition, Source Book Press, New York.

Aylmer, G.E. (1973), *The State's Servants: the Civil Service and the English Republic*, Routledge and Kegan Paul, London and Boston.

Ballaster, Ros (1992), *Seductive forms: women's amatory fiction from 1684 to 1740*, Clarendon Press, Oxford.

Barker, Felix, and Peter Jackson (1992), *The History of London in Maps*, Cross River Press, New York, London, Paris.

Bernikow, Louise ed. (1974), *The World Split Open: four Centuries of Women Poets in England and America, 1552-1950*, Vintage Books, London.

Boulton, Jeremy (1990), 'London widowhood revisited: the decline of female remarriage in the seventeenth and early eighteenth centuries', *Continuity and Change*, vol. 5 no. 3.

Boyce, Benjamin (1955), *The Polemic Character 1640-1661: a chapter in English literary history*, University of Nebraska Press, Lincoln.

Boyce, Benjamin (1967), *The Theophrastan Character in England to 1642*, Cass, London.

Burke, John and John Bernard Burke (1838), *A Genealogical and Heraldic History of the Extinct and Dormant Baronetcies of England, Ireland, and Scotland*, Scott, Webster and Geary, London.

Burke, Sir Bernard and Ashworth P. Burke (1906), *A Genealogical and Heraldic History of the Landed Gentry; or, Commoners of Great Britain and Ireland ...*, 11th edition, Harrison, London.

C., G.E. ed. (1900-06) *The Complete Baronetage*, 5 vols, W. Pollard and Co., Exeter.

C., G.E. ed. (1910, 1969), *The Complete Peerage of England, Scotland, Ireland, Great Britiain, and the United Kingdom ...*, St Catherine's Press, London.

Chalmers, Hero (1992), '"The Person I am, or What they Made me to be": the construction of the feminine subject in the autobiographies of Mary Carleton', in Brant, Clare and Diane Purkiss (eds), *Women, Texts and Histories 1575-1760*, Routledge, London.

Chapman, Colin R. (1992), *Ecclesiastical Courts, their Officials and their Records*, Lochin Publications, Dursley.

Coke, Edward (1629), *The First Part of the Institutes of the Lawes of England. Or, a commentarie vpon Littleton, not the name of a Lawyer onely, but of the Law it self*, 2nd edition, John More, London.

Conset, Henry (1685), *Practice of the Spiritual or Ecclesiastical Courts*, T. Basset, London.

Davis, Natalie Zemon (1987), *Fiction in the Archives: pardon tales and their tellers in sixteenth-century France*, Stanford University Press, Stanford.

Doody, Margaret Anne (1996), *The True Story of the Novel*, Rutgers University Press, New Brunswick, NJ.

Eden, Kathy (1986), *Poetic and Legal Fiction in the Aristotelian Tradition*, Princeton University Press, Princeton, NJ.

Ehrlich, J.W. (1959), *Ehrlich's Blackstone*, Nourse, San Carlos, California.

Erickson, Amy Louise (1990), 'Common Law *vs* Common Practice', *Economic History Review*, 2nd ser., vol. 43.

Erickson, Amy Louise (1993), *Women and Property in Early Modern England*, Routledge, London and New York.

Ezell, Margaret J.M. (1993a), 'Re-visioning the Restoration: or, how to stop obscuring early women writers', in Cox, Jeffrey N. and Larry J. Reynolds (eds), *New Historical Study*, Princeton University Press, Princeton, NJ.

Ezell, Margaret J.M. (1993b), *Writing Women's Literary History*, Johns Hopkins University Press, Baltimore and London.

[Fatio de Duillier, Nicolas] (1699), *Fruit-Walls Improved. By inclining them to the horizon: or, a way to build walls for fruit-trees; whereby they may receive more sun shine, and heat, than ordinary ...*, R. Everingham, London.

Foucault, Michel (1977), 'What is an author?' in Bouchard, Donald F. and Sherry Simon (trans. and ed.), Oxford University Press, Oxford.

Gardiner, Judith Ketan (1982), 'On Female Identity and Writing by Women', in Abel, Elizabeth (ed.), *Writing and Sexual Difference*, Harvester, Brighton.

Gilbert, Sir Geoffrey (1754, 1979), *The Law of Evidence*, facsimile, Garland, New York.

Ginzburg, Carlo (1986, 1989), *Clues, Myths, and the Historical Method*, trans. Tedeschi, John and Anne C., Johns Hopkins University Press, Baltimore and London.

Gordon, Lindall (1986), 'What's New in Women's History', in de Lauretis, Teresa (ed.), *Feminist Studies/Critical Studies*, University of Indiana Press, Bloomington.

Graham, Elspeth, Hilary Hinds, Elaine Hobby and Helen Wilcox ed.

(1989), *Her Own Life: autobiographical writings by seventeenth-century Englishwomen*, Routledge, London.
Grazebrook, George and John Paul Ryland (1889), *The Visitation of Shropshire. Taken in 1623*, Harleian Society, London.
Greer, Germaine et al. eds (1988), *Kissing the Rod: an anthology of seventeenth-century women's verse*, Virago, London.
Hacking, Ian (1975), *The Emergence of Probability*, Cambridge University Press, Cambridge.
Hale, Sir Matthew (1736, 1971), *Historia Placitorum Coronæ*, Classical English Law Texts, 2 vols, Professional Books, London.
Hale, Sir Matthew (1739), *The Analysis of the Law ...* 3rd edition, T. Waller, London.
Hale, Sir Matthew (1739, 1971), *The History of the Common Law of England*, 3rd edition, Gray, Charles M. (ed.), Chicago University Press, Chicago and London.
Haywood, Ian (1986), *The Making of History: a study of the literary forgeries of James MacPherson and Thomas Chatterton in relation to eighteenth-century ideas of history and fiction*, Fairleigh Dickinson, London and Toronto.
Helmholz, R.H. (1990), *Roman Canon Law in Reformation England*, Cambridge University Press, Cambridge.
Hobby, Elaine (1988), *Virtue of Necessity: English women's writing 1649-88*, Virago, London.
Hyde, Ralph ed. (1981), *The A to Z of Georgian London*, Lympne Castle, Kent, for the London Topographical Society, London.
Ingram, Martin (1987), *Church Courts, Sex and Marriage in England, 1570-1640*, Cambridge University Press, Cambridge.
Jackson, J. (1969), *The Formation and Annulment of Marriage*, 2nd edition, Butterworth, London.
Ketton-Cremer, R.W. (1944), *Norfolk Portraits*, Faber, London.
Lanser, Susan Sniader (1994), *Fictions of Authority: women writers and narrative voice*, Cornell University Press, Ithaca and London.
Le Neve's Pedigrees of the Knights made by King Charles II, and King James II, King William II and Queen Mary, King William Alone, and Queen Anne (1873), Marshall, George W. (ed.), Harleian Society, London.
Lillywhite, Bryant (1963), *London Coffee Houses*, Allen and Unwin, London.
Locke, John (1976), *An Essay Concerning Human Understanding*, Yolton, John (ed.), Everyman's Library, Dent, London.
Lyons, John O. (1978), *The Invention of the self: the hinge of consciousness in the eighteenth century*, Southern Illinois University Press, Carbondale and Edwardsville.
Markley, Robert (1987), 'Sentimentality as Performance:

Shaftesbury, Sterne, and the theatrics of virtue', in Nussbaum, Felicity and Laura Brown (eds), *The New Eighteenth Century*, Methuen, London.

Marsh, Christopher W. (1994), *The Family of Love in English Society, 1550-1630*, Cambridge University Press, Cambridge.

McKeon, Michael (1987), *The Origins of the English Novel 1600-1740*, Johns Hopkins University Press, Baltimore and London.

Nelson, William (1714, 1978), *Lex Testamentaria: or, a compendious system of all the laws of England, as well before the Statute of Henry VIII as since, concerning last wills and testaments. ...*, reprinted J. Nutt, London.

New Remarks of London; a survey of the cities of London and Westminster ... (1732), E. Midwinter, London.

Noble, Mark (1784), *Memoirs of the Protectorate-House of Cromwell ...*, 2 vols, Pearson and Rollason, Birmingham.

North, Roger (1972), *Lives of the Norths*, Jessopp, A. ed. (1890); reprinted Mackerness, E. (ed.), Greg, New York.

North, Roger (1995), *The Life of the Lord Keeper North*, Chan, Mary (ed.), The Edwin Mellen Press, Lewiston and Lampeter.

O'Donnell, Sheryl (1984), '"My Idea in Your Mind": John Locke and Damaris Cudworth Masham', in Perry, Ruth and Martine Brownley (eds), *Mothering the Mind*, Holmes and Meier, New York.

Ogg, David (1955), *England in the Reigns of James II and William III*, Oxford University Press, Oxford.

Patey, Douglas Lane (1984), *Probability and Literary Form: philosophic theory and literary practice in the Augustan age*, Cambridge University Press, Cambridge.

Perry, Ruth (1980), *Women, Letters, and the Novel*, AMS Press, New York.

Purvis, J.S. (1953), *An Introduction to Ecclesiastical Records*, St Anthony's Press, London.

Richardson, Samuel (1985), *Clarissa: or the history of a young lady*, Ross, Angus (ed.), Penguin Books, Harmondsworth.

Rose, Mary Beth (1986), 'Gender, Genre, and History: seventeenth-century English women and the art of autobiography', in Rose, Mary Beth (ed.), *Women in the Middle Ages and the Renaissance: literary and historical perspectives*, Syracuse University Press, Syracuse.

Shapin, Steven (1994), *A Social History of Truth: civility and science in seventeenth-century England*, University of Chicago Press, Chicago and London.

Shapiro, Barbara J. (1983), *Probability and Certainty in Seventeenth-Century England*, Princeton University Press, Princeton, NJ.

Shapiro, Barbara J. (1991), *'Beyond Reasonable Doubt' and 'Probable Cause': historical perspectives on the Ango-American law of evidence*, University of California Press, Berkeley.
Shaw, William A. (1906), *The Knights of England*, 2 vols, n.p., London.
Smeed, J.W. (1985), *The Theophrastan 'Character': a history of a literary genre*, Oxford University Press, Oxford.
Spacks, Patricia Meyer (1988), 'Female Rhetorics', in Benstock, Shari (ed.), *The Private Self: theory and practice of women's autobiographical writings*, Routledge, London.
Speck, W.A. (1988), *Reluctant Revolutionaries*, Oxford University Press, Oxford.
Squibb, G.D. (1977), *Doctors' Commons: a history of the College of Advocates and Doctors of Law*, Clarendon Press, Oxford.
Staves, Susan (1990), *Married Women's Separate Property in England, 1660-1833*, Harvard University Press, Cambridge, Mass., and London.
Stone, Lawrence (1979), *The Family, Sex and Marriage in England 1500-1800*, revised edition, Penguin Books, Harmondsworth.
Stone, Lawrence (1992), *Uncertain Unions: marriage in England 1660-1753*, Clarendon Press, Oxford.
Taylor, Charles (1989), *Sources of the Self: the making of modern identity*, Cambridge University Press, Cambridge.
Todd, Barbara J. (1985), 'The Remarrying Widow: a stereotype reconsidered', in Prior, Mary (ed.), *Women in English Society 1500-1800*, Methuen, London.
Todd, Barbara J. (1994), 'Demographic Determinism and Female Agency: the remarrying widow reconsidered ... again', *Continuity and Change*, vol. 9 no. 3.
Usher, Roland G. (1913), *The Rise and Fall of the High Commission*, Oxford University Press, Oxford.
Warner, William Beatty (1979), *Reading 'Clarissa': the struggles of interpretation*, Yale University Press, New Haven and London.
Weinreb, Ben and Christopher Hibbert (1993), *The London Encyclopaedia*, Macmillan, London.
Welsh, Alexander (1992), *Strong Representations: narrative and circumstantial evidence in England*, Johns Hopkins University Press, Baltimore and London.
White, Hayden (1987), *The Content of the Form: narrative discourse and historical representation*, Johns Hopkins University Press, Baltimore and London.
Whitmore of Apley Park: visitation of Shropshire ... 1623 (1889), Harleian Society Publications, London.
Würzbach, Natascha (1969), *The Novel in Letters: epistolary fiction*

in the early English novel 1678-1740, Routledge, London.

Zimbardo, Rose (1986), *A Mirror to Nature: transformations in drama and aesthetics 1660-1732*, University Press of Kentucky, Lexington.

Zomchick, John P. (1986), 'Tame Spirits, Brave Fellows, and the Web of Law: Robert Lovelace's legalistic Conscience', *ELH*, vol. 53.

Index of Names and Places

Banbury 54
Barret, Anne ('Nan') 35, 37
Bately, Mr (apothecary) 34, 54
Beaufort, duke and duchess of 42
Beddingfield, Henry 98
Bedford House 14
Bertie, Peregrine 37, 40, 44
Billber, Thomas ('a butcher') 45
Billingsgate 67
Bolns ('a butcher') 58
Brabazon, Lady Elizabeth ('Lady Betty') 30, 66
Brethren 93
Brettenham (Suffolk) 23, 27, 29, 34, 46, 47, 49, 52, 54, 60, 63, 69, 88
Bromsgrove market 58
Bury St Edmunds (Suffolk) 34, 54, 59, 74, 94
Butler, Samuel (author of *Hudibras*) 76

Callis 83
Catledge (Kirtling, Suffolk) 26, 70, 74, 75, 76, 101, 102
Charing Cross 101, 102
Chute, Elizabeth ('Betsy') 35
Chute, Thomas 2, 19, 24, 63, 64, 65, 66, 67
Closbrooke, Mr 54
'coffe[e] house neer Whitehall' 72
Coot, Sir Philip (of Ireland) 30
Covent Garden 102

Dacres, Lady Dorothy 77, 81, 82, 83, 86, 87, 88, 89, 91, 92, 93
Danvers, (Mr) 41, 59, 68, 70, 87
Darcy, Sir Thomas 84
Davey, Sir Thomas 89
de Vaux, Sir Theodore 41, 46, 51, 69, 74, 82, 87
Dixe, Thomas ('of Oxon') 46
Doctors' Commons 85, 99
Dog Tavern in Drury Lane 72-3

Enfield 83-4
Exton, Sir Thomas 99

Foley, Anne (Elizabeth's sister) 34, 46, 58
Foley (Folie), Sir Robert 43, 46, 58, 97
Fortescue, John 43, 58
Foynes (Fynes), Mistress 25

Goodwin, Mrs Susan 95

Hanwell (Oxfordshire) 6, 18, 20, 49
Harvey, Lady 102
Harvey, Mr 59
Hawkens, Mr 46
Hollis, Lord 92
Holytown 52, 59
Howard, Mary 68
Hughburne, Sir John 45, 58

Ipsley 43

J., Mat. 42
James II (king of England) 7, 8, 10, 13, 18, 21, 50, 73, 99, 100, 103

king, *see* James II
King, Captain 52, 59
King's Square (*see also* Soho Square) 7, 33

'Lady Jane' 92
Lane, Mrs 53, 54
Lawly, Sir Francis 1
Lawly, John ('uncle') 35, 44
Leicester Fields 5, 24, 51, 64
Lely, (?John) 84
Lichfield Cathedral 1
Lincolnshire 41
Long, Mr 30
'Lord O' (Lord North) 76, 77
Low, 'mother' 92

Man's Coffee House 101, 102
Mascall, Mrs 92
Middle Temple 10, 12, 33, 45, 58, 59, 67, 70, 72, 73, 92
Mildenhall (Suffolk) 48

Neale (Neal), Mr 34, 35, 37, 41, 47, 59, 68, 69, 70, 74, 75, 76, 84
Newmarket 101
North, Mrs 86
North, Anne (Elizabeth's mother) 39
North, Lady Anne (wife of Sir Dudley) 1, 20, 34, 36, 44, 60, 94, 102
North, Charles (Lord North and Grey) 1, 2, 3, 4, 5, 6, 7, 8, 9, 10, 11, 12, 13, 14, 18-19, 21, 22, 24, 25, 26, 35, 36, 38, 39, 40-2, 44, 45, 47, 48, 49-51, 52, 53, 54-7, 59, 60, 61, 62, 63, 65, 67, 69, 71-2, 73, 74, 76-9, 81-2, 86, 91, 96, 97, 100
North, Sir Dudley 1, 2, 10, 11, 12, 13, 15, 18-23, 27-32, 34-6,38, 39, 40, 42, 43-5, 46, 52-6, 59, 60-3, 64, 67, 69, 70, 73, 79-80, 81, 88
North, Dudley (son of Sir Dudley and Elizabeth's godson) 6, 36, 60, 94
North, Sir Francis (Lord Keeper) 6, 28, 41, 86, 89
North, Sir Henry 48, 55, 59, 73, 83
North, Lady Katharine (wife of Charles North) 1, 2, 3, 4, 6, 7, 9, 18-20, 21, 22, 23, 24, 25, 26, 27, 35, 36, 37, 65, 69, 91, 93, 102
North, Mountague 1, 9, 10, 15, 23, 36, 43-4, 45, 46, 47-8, 52-3, 54, 56, 63, 64, 68, 70, 71-2, 73, 76, 77, 78, 84, 88, 94
North, Roger 1-2, 9-14, 15-17, 21, 27, 32, 36, 37-9, 39-43, 45, 46, 47, 48, 50, 51-2, 54, 56, 58, 59, 60-7, 69-71, 72, 73, 75-84, 86, 87, 88-92, 94, 97, 98, 100, 102, 103

Oliver, Mr 43
Oxenbridge, Clement 95
Oxford 46
Oxfordshire 23

Paston, Thomas (brother to the 2nd Earl of Yarmouth) 98, 99, 101, 102
Paston, William (2nd Earl of Yarmouth) 2, 33, 96, 97, 98, 99, 101, 102, 103

Peterborough (Peterborrow), Lady 98
Philander 94
Powis, Lord 4
Plumstead, Mr 34, 36, 69

Rawlins, Captain Thomas 98, 99, 102
Russell, Lady 94

Secomb, Mr 102
Shaftesbury, Lady (Dorothy, wife of Antony Ashley Cooper 2nd Earl of Shaftesbury) 50, 73
Shafteswell, 95
Soho Buildings 7
Soho Square (*see also* King's Square) 33, 41, 85
Soresbye (Sowsby), Mr 34, 37, 68, 69, 84, 88
Sp. [Spencer], Mrs 82
Spencer family 10, 18, 49, 65
Spencer, Mr (of Hanwell, Robert Spencer's father) 18
Spencer, Mr (of Hanwell, the elder brother) 10, 18, 20
Spencer, Robert (2nd Earl of Sunderland) 4, 10, 13, 20, 38, 40, 90, 95, 98
Spencer, Robert ('the pretender') 1, 2, 3, 4, 5, 6, 9, 10, 11, 12, 13, 14, 16, 17, 18, 19, 20, 21, 22, 23-7, 36-7, 38, 40-2, 47-8, 49-51, 53, 54, 55, 56-7, 60-3, 64-7, 69, 71, 72, 73-4, 77, 78, 79, 80, 81, 85, 87, 90, 95, 96, 97, 98-100, 101, 102
Spencer, Mrs (mother of Robert Spencer) 6
Spycer, Dame 94
St Anne's Church 11,
St Johns, Lady 90
Stourbridge (Worcestershire) 42, 43, 45, 52, 58
Stowmarket (Suffolk) 76
Sussex, Lord 90
Swallow Street 102

Tenison, Dr 14, 30
Thorold, Lady (mother to Sir John) 15
Thorold, Sir Anthony 16

Thorold, Sir John 15-17, 35, 40, 41, 53, 55, 57, 60, 61, 71, 78
Thorold, Sir William 16
Tiverts, Lady 69
Tooting 1, 2, 4, 5, 9, 19, 21, 24, 27, 38, 49, 57, 65, 96
Tyviott (Teviot), Lord 50, 73

'unknowne freind' 70, 72-3, 75-6, 84

Wenyeve, Lady Christina (wife of Sir George) 34, 37, 44, 47, 59, 74, 86, 92
Wenyeve, Sir George 22, 34, 37, 39, 44, 47, 48, 51, 54, 59, 60, 63, 64, 68, 74, 92
Westminster Hall 5, 37, 40, 64
White, Francis 94-5
Winchrest, Mr 46

Winter 87
Wiseman, Lady Elizabeth 1, 2-8, 9, 10, 11, 14, 16-17, 18-22, 23-32, 33, 34, 36, 37 9, 10 5, 46, 47, 49-51, 53, 54, 56-7, 58, 59, 60-3, 65, 66, 67, 69, 71, 73, 75-81, 84, 88-92, 93, 96, 97, 99, 100, 103
Wiseman (Wyseman), Sir Richard 87
Wiseman, Sir Robert (Elizabeth's first husband) 85
Wright, Mr 52
Wroxton (Oxfordshire) 18, 41, 42, 43, 52
Wyet, Mr 95

Yarmouth, Earl of *see* Paston, William